The Sensual Philosophy

The Sensual Philosophy

Joyce and the Aesthetics of Mysticism

COLLEEN JAURRETCHE

The University of Wisconsin Press

The University of Wisconsin Press
2537 Daniels Street
Madison, Wisconsin 53718

3 Henrietta Street
London WC2E 8LU, England

Printed in the United States of America

Figures 2a and 2b are reprinted from *The Collected Works of St. John of the Cross,* translated by Kieran Kavanaugh and Otilio Rodriguez. Copyright © 1979, 1991 by Washington Province of Discalced Carmelites. ICS Publications, 2131 Lincoln Road, N.E., Washington, D.C. 20002. Figure 3 is reprinted from *Finnegans Wake* by James Joyce. Copyright © 1939 by James Joyce, copyright renewed 1967 by Giorgio Joyce and Lucia Joyce. Used by permission of Viking Penguin, a division of Penguin Books USA, Inc., and Faber & Faber.

Library of Congress Cataloging-in-Publication Data
Jaurretche, Colleen.
    The sensual philosophy : Joyce and the aesthetics of mysticism /
Colleen Jaurretche.
        168 pp.   cm.
    Includes bibliographical references (p.) and index.
    ISBN 0-299-15620-6 (cloth)
    1. Joyce, James, 1882–1941—Aesthetics.   2. Joyce, James,
1882–1941—Knowledge—Mysticism.   3. Medievalism—Ireland—
History—20th century.   4. Mysticism—History—Middle Ages,
600–1500.   5. Senses and sensation in literature.   6. Aesthetics,
Modern—20th century.   7. Middle Ages in literature.   8. Mysticism
in literature.   9. Aesthetics, Medieval.   I. Title.
PR6019.O9Z6455   1997
823'.912—dc21   97-15598

To Daddy, with love

Contents

Figures

Acknowledgments

My first and greatest thanks are due to Jack Kolb for introducing me to Joyce and enabling me to contemplate (and complete) this project. His caring attention and friendship have sustained me through every phase of its writing. In many ways I owe the earliest origins of this book to V. A. Kolve, who instilled a desire to understand the beauty of the Middle Ages and a reluctance to abandon its study. John Bishop, immanently present in this study, first pointed my enthusiasm toward the subject of mysticism. His "lingerous longerous" thoughts on Joyce, as well as his cheering humor, have illuminated many darknesses when I was "thrust from the light, apophotorejected" (*FW*, 251). I thank Vince Cheng for his friendship, guidance, and good spirits. Through his generosity the Southern California Finnegans Wake Group has continued in its combination of merriment and serious study; without such support I would never have attempted to "scale the summit." Margot Norris has graciously read drafts and supported my efforts in every way, and numerous other Joyceans have offered me their wisdom and conviviality. I especially thank Michael Patrick Gillespie and Mary Reynolds for their helpful advice in preparing the manuscript for publication. Finally I wish to thank the Huntington Library for accommodating my research needs in the loveliest of settings, and Mary Elizabeth Braun and all at the University of Wisconsin Press for putting my efforts into print.

I must thank those friends who have helped and listened for many years, including: Laura Grimes, Sue Johnson, Lisa Boore Lambert, Patricia Moisan, John Murphy, Tim Murphy, Patricia Juliana Smith, Robby Sproul, Elisa Vandernoot, all Wakegroup members past and present. But my greatest indebtedness is to my family, who lavished love, patience, and attention through all stages of this project: to Kathy, Grandma, Lisa, Sidney, and Sandy, for all their support; to baby Ryan for putting up with some mighty odd bedtime stories; to my husband

Geoff for his understanding and sense of humor. To Rita, to whom things have often recircled, I have fulfilled a promise. And to Daddy, for everything, I dedicate this book—"Loud, heap miseries upon us yet entwine our arts with laughters low!" (*FW*, 259.7).

Abbreviations

CW   James Joyce. *Critical Writings.* Ed. Ellsworth Mason and Richard Ellmann. Ithaca: Cornell University Press, 1989.

D   James Joyce. *Dubliners.* New York: Viking, 1961.

FW   James Joyce. *Finnegans Wake.* New York: Penguin, 1967.

NCE   *New Catholic Encyclopedia.* Ed. William J. McDonald. New York: McGraw-Hill, 1967.

ODCC   *Oxford Dictionary of the Christian Church.* Ed. F. L. Cross. London: Oxford, 1974.

P   James Joyce. *A Portrait of the Artist as a Young Man.* New York: Viking, 1964.

SH   James Joyce. *Stephen Hero.* New York: New Directions, 1944.

U   James Joyce. *Ulysses.* New York: Random House, 1986.

The Sensual Philosophy

Introduction

In the Buginning

Joyce constantly invites us to see the world as enlivened by the private life of the mind. Stephen thinks about this interior life as the "light shining in darkness which darkness cannot comprehend" (U, 21), enigmatic wording suggestive of mental experience that escapes ordinary comprehension. Joyce liked the obscurely resonant phrase with origins in the theology of the early mystics because it illumines the opaque epistemology of the mind apparent in his fictions of day and night. Joyce's interest in theological history and practice comes as no surprise; critics have long used it as evidence of both Joyce's belief and his unbelief. But to consider Joyce's sense of the origins and beginnings of theology highlights the greater mystery surrounding his idea of mystery itself: how do we come to knowledge? He finds an answer to this question inherent in mystical theology's idea of God and its consequent model of the human mind. Joyce sees phenomenological processes in terms of the medieval mystical tradition, which understands God as outside of time, space, and conceptual thought altogether, and thus concerns itself with the philosophical problem of coming to divine knowledge. For Joyce this tradition suggests the most powerful of analogies to the creating, artistic mind, capable of redefining categories of truth and beauty in the presence of dark uncertainty. Against conceptual emptiness and philosophic incertitude, Joyce articulates aesthetic ideas in cognitive terms. He points to medieval religious culture to explain qualities of modern awareness and representation, finding in mystical theology an integrated image of body and mind suggestive of his own sense of the inward, subjective moment of creation.

But how does Joyce come to a consideration of theology as a model for art? Stories of his relationship to the Catholic Church emphasize his rejection of traditional authority yet fondness for ritual and beauty. The congruencies between Joyce's youth and Stephen Dedalus' piety are well known: he really did follow devotions to the Virgin Mary, pray at the altar in the wood, consider and reject the priesthood (Ellmann, *James Joyce*, 30). And his concept of art really did evolve from the generative image of the girl on the beach whose "mortal youth and beauty" (*P*, 172) solidified his sense that art and life, not art and religion, are one. The facts of his troubled yet invigorated relationship to the Church underlie the premise of Mary Reynolds' *Joyce and Dante: The Shaping Imagination* and Beryl Schlossmann's *Joyce's Catholic Comedy of Language*, studies of Joyce's accommodation of Catholicism to his artistic disposition. These books form a part of the learned critical tradition that analyzes Joyce's confluence of religious culture and aesthetics in terms of medieval scholasticism, Jesuit tradition, and postmodern theory, each in its own way defining the elusive, "supersaturated" qualities of his imagination.

In *Joyce and Aquinas*, William T. Noon inaugurates discussion of Joyce's debt to medieval culture as one feature of his adaptation of theology to artistic purposes. Noon states that Joyce builds upon Aquinas' concept of beauty as it exists in the mind, and therefore in the subjectivity of the senses. This "applied Aquinas" furnishes a rationalistic explanation for the objective qualities of reality figured in *Portrait* and *Ulysses*. As a consequence Noon primarily searches for concepts suggestive of exteriority, finding for example in Stephen's "flight from reality" in *Portrait* an "aesthetic nightmare and religious void." In briefly considering the influence of mysticism, he accurately recognizes that Stephen is "no mystic" but does not remark any relationship between "religious void" and the aesthetic that Stephen derives from it (Noon, 99). Similarly Kevin Sullivan in *Joyce among the Jesuits* wishes to show Joyce's essential complicity with Jesuit thought. He avoids the subject of Joyce's religious disposition, instead treating the tension between faith and doubt in dualistic terms by figuring the latter as a void of knowledge. Sullivan comes directly to the concept of mysticism, if only briefly. He quotes Gorman's biography, which records that the Homeric material appealed to Joyce because of its "mysticism" (Sullivan, 95). Sullivan discounts the concept of mysticism because of its implied asceticism—he reasons that Joyce was only twelve upon first looking into Lamb's *Ulysses*—and instead looks to the appeal of allegorical and occulted meaning to explain the anecdote. Contemporary with Noon and Sullivan, Morse writes in *The Sympathetic Alien: James Joyce and Catholicism* that for Joyce the mystical contribution to theology lay in its nondiscursive logic and emphasis upon individual experience, the only evidence of which is Stephen's dream in *Portrait*'s final chapter.

More recently Robert Boyle's *James Joyce's Pauline Vision* embraces the union of art and theology in many ways and approaches the context of mysticism in its own right. Boyle argues that Joyce expresses intuitive and nonrational reality as part of the act of grace that expands the limits of the mind and enables knowledge of God. He sees religious enthusiasm and intuition connected in Joyce, to the purpose of revealing the "ineffable mystery" at the heart of his work (Boyle, ix). What follows is a beautifully expressed call to avoid rational certitude and, like Shakespeare and Hopkins, engage an imaginative world in which "apprehension replaces comprehension" (Boyle, 8). As a consequence Boyle responds positively to the idea of absence of knowledge in matters holy and the necessity of epistemological instability at the heart of religious and artistic vision. His work begins to suggest what Joyce may have meant in writing to his son Giorgio: "My eyes are tired. For over half a century, they have gazed into nullity where they have found a lovely nothing" (Ellmann, *Collected Letters*, 3:358, 361).

The critical study of Joyce's indebtedness to religious culture follows his gaze into precisely those "voids" of experience otherwise unaccounted for in the history of the mind and its search for knowing. Umberto Eco, for example, pursues medieval aesthetics as Joyce's greatest linguistic determinant. The work of others, most immediately Eliot Gose, Jean-Michel Rabaté, and Susan Shaw Sailer, directly addresses concepts of absence. John Bishop argues for the nullities of night present within the body as the *Wake*'s most compelling subject. In letters, essays, and fiction Joyce looks to the lovely nothingness of mystical theology as particularly descriptive of those real absences of body and mind as they shape his art. Most persuasively, Joyce named John of the Cross, made Doctor Mysticus in 1926, as one of four progenitors of the *Wake*'s night, and we must shun no light shining in that particular darkness.

Chapter 1 establishes Joyce's artistic investment in mysticism, defining at length the history and aesthetic concepts of the strain that appealed to him. Joyce was especially drawn to the tradition begun by Dionysius the Areopagite. He and his inheritors were intensely devoted to an interior exploration of consciousness and especially concerned with God's ineffability. In brief, to follow Bernard McGinn, the term "mysticism" denotes a "sense of the presence of God," and the specific tradition that appeals to Joyce demands intense introspection. From the writing of *Critical Essays* through the composition of *Finnegans Wake*, Joyce exploits this apophatic, or negative, theology for the philosophical, psychological, and aesthetic advantages of a literature whose focus lies in the quieting of the mind and senses. For Joyce, as for John of the Cross, this introspection holds a mirror, darkly, to consciousness and its relationship to the senses as they mediate inner and outer worlds. For example, negative mysticism implies a remove from sensory impressions the better to "see" the object of its study, and the visual metaphor of sight itself demonstrates the difficulty of translating such a maneuver into words. Of equal perplexity is the insistence upon "knowing" a deity without attributes. The literary problems, then, of describing this negative awareness or knowledge mimic other difficulites in accurately correlating the world without with the world within—very stimulating to a writer already preoccupied with the alterities of experience and the technical difficulties of putting them into words. Joyce finds in these literary questions their own answers, and the literary solution to a few problems of his own. In a fundamental way Joyce looks to mysticism's inherent, if paradoxical, recourse to the world of the senses as they shape perception and form consciousness. He looks to the cognitive relationships set forth in the mystical texts to surmount the division of body and mind and reinvest the mystical phenomena of search and inquiry from the discovery of God to the mental exploration of sensuality and art.

The second chapter pursues the intellectual valency of mysticism and its shaping contribution to the literary imagination as a model for art in the writing of the late nineteenth century, the period of modernism's infancy and Joyce's coming of age. This chapter too stands preparatory to anything else. It focuses upon Joyce's critical writings in their understanding of the late nineteenth century's involvement in mystical thought as a model for an analysis of the writings of Walter Pater, Francis Thompson, James Thomson, and Gerard Manley Hopkins. Joyce's intellectual background and milieu, whether he knew it or not, appropriated mystical ideas to literary ends, thus articulating an increasingly modern sense of the nature of perception and consciousness itself. In so doing these writers shifted the original mystical desire for God to the exploration of private interiority. This quest for meaning takes the practical shape of a literature intent upon breaking down the divisions of mental and physical experience in ways that immediately anticipate the solipsism of *Portrait*, whose experiment with the experiential language of mysticism is the subject of chapter 3.

In any book each part bears upon another. Throughout it is my intention to show an intrinsic development in Joyce's writing that renders the *Wake* fundamentally determined by the aesthetic structures of mysticism in its presentation of consciousness and relentless search for knowledge. To that end the fourth chapter, on *Ulysses*, examines perception's mystical determinants in their bearing upon the creating mind through Joyce's indebtedness to Jewish and Christian traditions of knowing. As a book of diurnal experience *Ulysses* focuses upon the conscious and subconscious acquisition of knowledge in art's creation. Joyce explicitly structures the philosophical resolution of mind and body mystically, thus reconstructing cognition and imagination in terms of the darker mysteries of the mind.

These mysteries are the essence of *Finnegans Wake*, whose pages are doused with the "thomistically drunk" (510.18) imagination of its author in his appropriation of the concepts of sensualized absence, darkness, and forgetting. The nondiscursive logic of negative mysticism, insistent upon an alternative ontology, perfectly supports the rearranged perceptual, cognitive, and sensory abilities of the body which darkly contemplates the quality and meaning of ultimate knowledge. The *Wake* "idself" poses the question anterior to knowledge, "where did thots come from?" (*FW*, 597.25). The philosophical terms of mysticism guide the nocturnal consciousness to answer through an obscure meshing of sensual subjectivity and radical uncertainty, leading to a comical surety that the "aristmystic unsaid" (293.18) indeed shines a light in darkness that only darkness can comprehend. Joyce invites us through letter and word to an understanding of that darkness in its mystical figuration in the hope that we may become greater participants in the play of his world without end.

1

Medieval Abstrusiosities
The Negative Mystical Tradition

To Joyce the concepts of mystical theology determine creativity and art through a complex and paradoxical interrelation of body and mind, perception and sense. From his youthful critical writings to *Finnegans Wake* Joyce echoes, sometimes in earnest, sometimes in the earnestness of verbal play, the texts and authors of the Christian mystical tradition from Dionysius the Areopagite to Saint John of the Cross as the means by which he understands intellectual cognition and artistic representation. Stephen thinks to himself in "Proteus": "We don't want any of your medieval abstrusiosities" (*U*, 38). The phrase and its call to plain words point to an intellectual and imaginative habit of mind that frames Joyce's concept of mental interiority in terms of medieval culture. Here and elsewhere Joyce draws from medieval literature his idea of thought itself and defines his philosophy of the mind within the epistemological structures of mysticism. He absorbs not only the metaphorical language but also the philosophical assumptions of that medieval mystical tradition which expresses its idea of God, and hence knowledge, in nondiscursive terms. This tradition ultimately leads to an exploration of darkness and unknowing through its use of conceptual absence, essential to Joyce's construction of (non)reality in *Finnegans Wake*. Arguably his most ambitious representation of psychology and consciousness, the *Wake* uses mystical writing to articulate central ideas of darkness and negation. In an unequivocal way Joyce wrote to Harriet Shaw Weaver in a letter dated 28 May 1929 that John of the Cross's *Dark Night of the Soul* ranks with the *Book of the Dead* as the foremost text for the "treatment of the night" in *Finnegans Wake*. In fact, Joyce wished to commission a long critical essay about its influence, but his plans never came into being (Atherton, 192). John of the Cross's writing fulfills the ideals of the medieval negative mystical tradition. He figures his nocturnal search for God as cognitive abandonment, and Joyce adopts both his work and his potent mystical tradition to infuse his vocabulary with words and images of the night.

Joyce shows great enthusiasm for the tradition of John of the Cross at the satirical expense of his contemporaries' "mystical" interest in occultism and theosophy. Richard Ellmann notes that such ideas appeared, in Joyce's words, unable to "compare either from consistence, holiness or charity with a fifth-rate saint of the Catholic Church" (Ellmann, *James Joyce*, 99). Instead, as his brother Stanislaus remembers in *The Dublin Diary*, Joyce admired the mystics of the Catholic tradition: "They interest me. In my opinion, they are writing about a very real spiritual experience . . . and they went about it with a subtlety I don't find in many so-called psychological novels" (Ellmann, *James Joyce*, 108). His bias is clear; Joyce correlates mystical writing with the modern impulse to make art of the workings of the human mind and accords great psychological authenticity to the spiritual tradition.

A preliminary glance at Joyce's critical writing suggests the contours of his mystical appropriation. As early as his 1911 lecture on William Blake, Joyce displays his affinity for medieval culture and his understanding of mysticism's relevance to his aesthetic values. While he champions Blake as an artistic visionary, the essay's interest lies in Joyce's provocative observations about the influence of traditional mystical theology upon the arts. He idealizes the restructuring of ontology and cognition that occurs under the guidance of an at once radical and theological mind. According to the young Joyce, the imagination of Blake sees with the "eye of the mind" and hears with the "ear of the soul" to note oppression and injustice (*CW*, 215). The fusion of sense and spirit implicit in the metaphor conforms to Paul's words in 1 Corinthians 2:9 to the literal end of turning mystical insight to aesthetic reality. In a tone both eulogistic and triumphant Joyce remarks of Blake's psychic journeys: "The visions, multiplying, blind the sight; and toward the end of his mortal life, the unknown for which he had yearned covered him with the shadows of vast wings, and the angels with whom he conversed as an immortal with immortals hid him in the silence of their garments" (*CW*, 215). Blake, in Joyce's rhapsody, becomes a blind seer and transforms himself into the subject of his own contemplation, a divine being merged with the unknown. To Blake, as well as to Joyce, this transcendence denotes not only artistic inspiration but also reward for "spiritual rebellion" of a pacifist kind. Joyce finds Blake's radical politics and poetics congenial, particularly in their religious expression. He glories all the more in Blake's "undisciplined and visionary" qualities when he compares them with the orthodoxy and "stupefaction" of Francesco Suarez and Mariano de Talavera, names in *A Portrait of the Artist as a Young Man* that represent rejection of institutional authority and serve in the essay to emphasize the nature of Blake's religious insubordination. In describing Blake's death, Joyce again invokes the idea of radical rebellion, stating that the poet expired "singing, as always, of the ideal world, of truth, the intellect and the divinity of imagination" (*CW,* 220).

Joyce divides Blake's radical disposition into three categories, "the pathological, the theosophical and the artistic," in order to evaluate mysticism's effect upon his intellect. Joyce first rescues the work of artists from any insinuations of "madness," arguing instead that madness "in fact, is a medical term that can claim no more notice from the objective critic than he grants the charge of heresy raised by the theologian, or the charge of immorality raised by the police" (*CW,* 220). Joyce continues the assault upon the "happy fatuousness" of those who favor literal interpretation and material substance over philosophical speculation and ineffability, stating that the resulting death of "art and universal philosophy" occurs at the price of "a large part of the peripatetic system, all of medieval metaphysics, a whole branch of the immense symmetrical edifice constructed by the Angelic Doctor, St. Thomas Aquinas, Berkeley's idealism, and (what a combination) the skepticism that ends with Hume" (*CW,* 220). By reducing the charge of madness to a rhetorical category possessing no more truth value than law enforcement, where accusers create no art greater than "court stenography," Joyce simultaneously deconstructs both the Romantic ideology of the crazed artist and the primacy of the material and logical.

In place of logical systems Joyce suggests that the "theosophical" and the "artistic" features of Blake's personality are one. Joyce determines that Blake is "not a great mystic" yet analyzes his relationship to some aspects of mystical tradition, thus defining by contrast his sense of the subject. He begins as does some research contemporary to his time. By asserting that the "orient is the paternal home of mysticism" he understands the "vast cycles of spiritual activity and passivity" as the central concern of Eastern religious thought, barely penetrable to Western consciousness. Blake's spiritual resistance to occidental perception and comprehension, "ideational energy" that Joyce hesitates to dub thought, forms the basis for visionary and alchemical traditions whose resistance to traditional thinking strikes Joyce as similar to that of the mystics he admires. He here denies Blake's likeness to Paracelsus, Boehme, and

Swedenborg, claiming that Blake is less Eastern than his predecessors and therefore less objectionable. The passage turns upon Joyce's semantics; he returns for the sake of convenience to the term "theosophy" to discriminate between the "cycles of spiritual activity and passivity" and the expanded idea of the mind that he finds in the Western mystical tradition (*CW*, 220).

In this essay Joyce ultimately wishes to diminish Blake's private theology in favor of his poetic, which reveals the aesthetic possibilities of mysticism for the literary and visual imagination. In stating that Blake's "visionary faculty is directly connected with the artistic" (*CW*, 221), Joyce presents a measured response to mystical literature as a whole. While it seems to Joyce to require "the patience of a saint" to read most mystical and alchemical texts, Blake's reading permitted him "keenness of intellect with mystical feeling." Mental acuity, Joyce further states, "is almost completely lacking in mystical art." Considering Joyce's distinction between genius and the "court stenographer" school of creativity that results from an unintuitive grasp of reality, the initial appeal of mystical literature lies in its ability to provide an emotive context for art. In this connection Joyce first cites John of the Cross as "one of the few idealist artists worthy to stand with Blake," although he "never reveals either an innate sense of form or a coordinating force of the intellect in his book *The Dark Night of the Soul*, that cries and faints with such an ecstatic passion" (*CW*, 221). The "ecstatic passion" continues the "mystical feeling" necessary to art and, in Joyce's scheme, matters more than coherent but lifeless reason; the realm of the artist is that of the metaphysical. Joyce refines the link between art and metaphysics by suggesting that Blake benefits not only from visionary literature but also from pictorial art. He cites Blake's words on Michelangelo, "'one of the Gothic Artists who built the cathedrals in what we call the Dark Ages . . . of whom the world was not worthy.'" Michelangelo in his "formal precision" taught Blake "especially in some passages of prose collected in the fragments . . . the importance of the pure, clean line that evokes and creates the figure on the background of the uncreated void." In this moment Joyce abandons surface distinctions of print and art, aesthetics and theology, suggesting that the moment of creative insight parallels the construction of the universe. The mystical artist becomes the ultimate master of the *creatio ex nihilo*, reinvigorating the poetic imagination with intellectual structures of theology and the "power of the sensual philosophy" (*CW*, 221).

This fragmented essay concludes its description of mysticism's role in the making of literary art with an homage to Swedenborg and his

central image of angelic man in whom heaven resides. Joyce's enthusiasm for this idea lies primarily in the humanistic and erotic possibilities
of a creature infused with divinity, "animated in all his limbs by a fluid
angelic life that forever leaves and re-enters, systole and diastole of love
and wisdom" (CW, 221). The final paragraph describes the artistic effect
of the visual and visionary stimulus upon Blake by focusing upon the
negative mystical tradition as most potent for the production of art.
Blake, Joyce says, "killed the dragon of experience and natural wisdom, and, by minimizing space and time and denying the existence of
memory and the senses . . . tried to paint his works on the void of the
divine bosom." Time and space collapse and the nature of reality becomes the void, the uncreated subjectivity of the unconscious, the conscience and the canvas of the mind. Joyce accounts for this aesthetic by
turning to mystical theology: "Not with the eye, then, but beyond the
eye, the soul and the supreme love must look, because the eye, which
was born in the night while the soul was sleeping in rays of light, will
also die in the night." These optics of spirituality deny personality, affect, sensory apprehension, and reason, accepting the paradox of night
as the condition of both spiritual deprivation and enlightenment. This
is the theology of Dionysius the pseudo-Areopagite whose "De Divinis
Nominibus, arrives at the throne of God by denying and overcoming
every moral and metaphysical attribute, and falling into ecstasy before
the divine obscurity, before that unutterable immensity which precedes and encompasses the supreme knowledge in the eternal order"
(CW, 222). In this appropriation of theology as an aesthetic creed, the
artist-adept merges the transcendence of God with the primacy of creativity implicit in the very structure of this spiritual tradition: this is the
paradoxical void of possibility that at once limits human understanding
and celebrates lack as a positive value. In the culmination of this tradition John of the Cross will abandon his treatise in la noche dichosa—the
happy night of incomplete potentiality.

   While this early article on Blake by no means encompasses Joyce's
total response to the issues of artistry and inspiration, it does suggest
what he may have come to gain from consistent attention to the tradition of mystical theology. Dionysius, the author of Mystical Theology and
Divine Names, provides the earliest source and most powerful authority
for the metaphorical and intellectual constructions of darkness, loss,
and absence as the loci of divinity. By relinquishing the world of sense
and reason, the process of revelation and understanding becomes that
of describing the void. This spiritual knowledge, termed negative or
apophatic, comprises one of the main foundations of Christian mysti-

cism. Joyce attributes to this mystical tradition the ability to render cognitive absence as the highest form of spiritual and sensual expression, representing powerful alternative realities of the mind. The evolution of Joyce's work displays this particular sense of mystical understanding, from the religious enthusiasm and sensual discovery of *A Portrait of the Artist as a Young Man* to the meditation upon doubt and mortality of *Ulysses* and the "surrection" of ontology and embrace of night of *Finnegans Wake*. In his commitment to creating the figure of the mind on the uncreated background of the page Joyce infuses the structures of medieval culture and mysticism with the ability to surmount ordinary distinctions of being and knowing, mind and body, and sees in this philosophy the most radical form of representation.

This chapter will fix upon the elements of the negative mystical tradition that enable art and contribute to the overall theological relationship of darkness and understanding that shapes Joyce's presentation of the phenomenology of the mind. Knowledge of the medieval source materials in which he read deeply is crucial to grasping his construction of the mind and its relationship to perception, the first step toward Joyce's sensual philosophy. After all, "he's weird, I tell you, and middayevil down to his vegetable soul" (*FW*, 423.27).

Mysticism most properly takes its philosophical roots in the concept of mystery itself and the human propensity to grasp incertitude before comprehension. Bernard McGinn's definition of mysticism as "a sense of the presence of God" identifies the numinous quality of religious encounter but leaves open to individual tradition the means by which this happens. Joyce, ever mindful of the ineffability of creativity, explores the phenomenological qualities of the mind inherent in mysticism's construction of real presence as an analogy to the artistic experience. In Christian practice mysticism takes its origins from the earliest biblical texts of creation, prophecy, and revelation, as well as from Neoplatonic philosophy. Apophatic mysticism, sometimes called negative theology, defines that sense of presence through negation and denial, accepting the condition of nothingness as the most powerful ontological state. Thus mental interiority comprises the most supreme reality. Fundamentally different from the affective devotion, emotional expressiveness, and theology of love of Francis of Assisi or Theresa of Avila, the inwardness that typifies apophatic mystical experience nonetheless bases description of God in the realm of the senses. According to Eric Colledge, there really is no "pure mysticism" that exists without affective qualities (Colledge, 14). Because mystical expression contains elements of both affective and apophatic impulses, it carries the potential to express inward states of being through the senses, and this ability forms the basis for its relationship to art. In this movement from sense to concept the cognitive experience of God forms the basis for aesthetic theory. To Joyce that experience becomes the most universally human one of artistic self-discovery, as in the authorial consciousness of the *Wake*, "self exiled in upon his ego . . . writing the mystery of himsel" (*FW*, 184.6–10).

The origin of the apophatic strain begins with Plato. Andrew Louth identifies the Platonic impulse as one in which the soul, sensitive to beauty, seeks for God's "self-disclosure" in the "sleep of the mind" (Louth, 33). That self-disclosure is native to the soul's search for God and Joyce's quest for the illimitable night of the *Wake*'s sleeping consciousness. The quest for self-disclosure, both of God and of the individual, becomes the defining moment for the intellectual search of the mystic, both Platonic and medieval, and the condition of sleep suggests the physical and metaphorical state of greatest deprivation and enlightenment. This same sleep begets dreams of union with the divine, and Louth refines his Platonic root tracing against the contribution of Plotinus' "flight of the alone to the Alone." He suggests that the Greek contemplative tradition falls short of the Christian ideal; in Christian practice solitariness and isolation, while psychologically valid, fail to evoke the theology of union sought by mystics.

Dionysius the pseudo-Areopagite provides the earliest systematic meditation on the ineffability of God and the interiority of the mystical experience. Little is known about pseudo-Dionysius' identity. For centuries he was identified as Dionysius the Areopagite whom Paul converted to Christianity; however, internal evidence dates his work approximately five hundred years later. The confusion was deepened by his identification as Saint Denis, the patron of Paris. Subsequent scholarship proved he was neither, but earned him the name "pseudo" in front of his own freely chosen pseudonym, Dionysius, and contemporary scholars follow many variations on his name, including Denys. His corpus consists of four works, each of enormous importance to the development of Western theology: *Celestial Hierarchy, Ecclesiastical Hierarchy, Divine Names,* and *Mystical Theology.* These works profoundly influenced the aesthetics and philosophy of the Middle Ages and permanently inscribed their vision and understanding of God, especially, according to Paul Rorem, "with regard to Gothic architecture at the abbey church of Saint-Denis near Paris; Scholastic philosophy and theology, specifically that of Thomas Aquinas; the interpretation of the liturgy as a dramatic allegory; medieval mysticism . . . and the entire subject of negative, or apophatic theology" (Rorem, 3).

Dionysius explores how the mind comes to know obscurity. He presumes God's nature and aspect to be "hidden" and "secret" and therefore beyond ordinary comprehension. The nature of secrecy points to conceptual truths about the origins of knowledge as insurmountably muffled. He conveys the process of enlightenment, itself only a metaphor for a qualified appreciation of God, through his symbolism of light and dark, ascent and descent—omnipresent words that filter through all literature and fall, gracefully, through the obscure secrets of the *Wake*. Dionysius' fascination with dark and light parallels his search for self-disclosure figured as ascent and descent, or excursion and return. Of these patterns Rorem says Dionysius forms a "subjective epistemology . . . a cognitive exercise, dominated throughout by the right interpretation of the revealed names and symbols for God . . . and climaxed by the intentional abandonment of all such interpretations" (Rorem, 200). Dionysius' spiritual hermeneutics instruct Joyce in the incursively designed language of bodily sleep and mental acuity, thus conceptually reconstructing ordinary concepts of the perceiving mind.

This introspective reconstruction paradoxically occurs outside of the realm of language. In *Divine Names* Dionysius articulates the path to understanding: "in a manner surpassing speech and knowledge, we reach a union superior to anything available to us by way of our own abilities or activities in the realm of discourse or intellect" (pseudo-Dionysius, 49). In *Mystical Theology* speaking by denial, a rhetorical structure of negation that leads to neither being nor nonbeing, concludes with a theological explosion of apophasis wherein the "supreme cause of every conceptual thing is not itself conceptual." Dionysius figures negation as the absence of imagination, speech, understanding, power, life, substance, or time. The concept of the divine exists at a remove from its inspiration, "next to it, but never of it, for it is both beyond every assertion, being the perfect and unique cause of all things, and, by virtue of its preeminently simple and absolute nature, free of every limitation, beyond every limitation; it is also beyond every denial" (pseudo-Dionysius, 141). In this most astonishing statement apophatic knowledge equates the anagogic relation of imagination and creation to the "mysterious darkness of unknowing." This definition by negation eradicates any possibility of depicting God: "Just as the senses can neither grasp nor perceive the things of the mind, just as representation and shape cannot take in the simple and the shapeless, just as corporal form cannot lay hold of the intangible and incorporeal, by the

same standard of truth beings are surpassed by the infinity beyond being, intelligences by that oneness which is beyond intelligence . . . nor
can any words come up to the inexpressible Good, this One, this Source
of all unity, this supra-existent Being. Mind beyond mind, word beyond
speech, it is gathered up by no discourse, by no intuition, by no name"
(50). The resistance of God as Logos to any notion of fixity suggests, in
the most basic of ways, the fundamental inability of language ever to
represent reality with absolute accuracy, or of the human mind ever to
know with certainty. It points to the value of rhetoric in spite of its objection to naming in a system of words that simultaneously resist and
define experience.

Considering the paradox inherent within Dionysius' writing, how
does he narrate conscious knowledge, of God or anything else? The
epistemological indeterminacy created by the lack of referents for God
or the individual demands a way of writing "the sleep of the mind"
without violating its insubstantiality. In his recourse to metaphorical
language Dionysius frequently covers God with clouds, or refers to
Moses' excursion to and return from the mount, or employs the imagery of light inherent in the burning bush (a story that he popularized for contemplative use) to suggest that obscurity and ineffability.
Wolfgang Riehle in his linguistic discussion of mystical writing observes that such metaphorical language transcends words to constitute
spiritual acts unto themselves (Riehle, 104). Dionysius' recourse to the
metaphorical language and human experience reinvests the senses with
the power of knowledge and spiritual identification. While he assumes
the essential inadequacy of language to the mystical experience, nonetheless he communicates the understanding of the senses through the
medium of words.

This sensual understanding, Joyce's "sensual philosophy," forms the
basis of the Dionysian contribution to aesthetic theory. The incarnation
itself necessitates a mode of discourse that acknowledges the importance of the body and the senses as a vehicle for meaning. Dionysius
states that the "Trinity holds within a shared undifferentiated unity its
supra-essential subsistence," which through grace becomes divided
and incarnate. The division of the Trinity into the distinctness of Christ
becomes the primary "instance of differentiation" (pseudo-Dionysius,
61) or descent into personality, substance, and corporal reality of human existence. This maneuvre from Word to word embodies "the most
evident idea in theology, namely, the sacred incarnation of Jesus for our
sakes" (65). The pattern of the Incarnation holds within it the conceptual and metaphorical paradoxes of the answers of theology for ques-

tions of being and expression. According to Louth the relationship of negative theology to the moment of expression lies in Dionysius' concept of symbols: "All symbols and images are to be denied to God; none, not even lofty and spiritual ones are ultimately privileged . . . all symbols and images may be affirmed of him . . . Apophatic theology and symbolic theology—or iconic theology—are two sides of the same coin" (Louth, 178). The senses that Dionysius writes of are closer to Augustine's spiritual senses than to a literal rendering of sight, sound, and touch. Augustine will later join with Dionysius to emphasize the "eye of the heart" as the quintessential mystical image of spiritual perception. This eye of the heart gazes inward to behold the nature of nothingness and insubstantiality, looking to articulate "from the field of sensual contemplation" a language that points out that "it is only in a sensuality which is, as it were, transposed and sublimated, that man is able to have spiritual experiences at all" (Riehle, 3). To Dionysius the detached sleep of the mind looks with the eye of the heart upon desire itself. To Joyce the dreamer of *Finnegans Wake* sleeps "heartsoul dormant mid shadowed landscape" (*FW*, 471.2) to receive knowledge by body and mind.

Metaphors of spiritual sight dominate Dionysius' symbols for God. Indeed his understanding of the importance of visuality so influenced the contemplative practice of the Middle Ages that the process of the "visio Dei" itself was figured in visual terms. The north wall of Chartres depicts in painting several women pursuing different stages of contemplation. At the summit of enlightenment the figure of a woman looks upward, beholding with the sense of sight the source of illumination (Riehle, 122). To the theology of Dionysius and the medieval aesthetic theory that he shaped, visual perception formed the core of inward understanding through outward analogy. The Middle Ages distinguished three different kinds of vision. In the first level one physically perceives objects, while in the second perception is absent and the imagination takes over, as in the state of sleep, or prayer. The third stage of perception is entirely spiritual, lacking in any physical corollary for mental experience. In its transcendence of various stages of apprehension Dionysius' "visio Dei" elegantly unites mind and body despite the paradox inherent in his theology. Thus Bernard McGinn joins with Hans Urs von Balthasar "in insisting that the whole tenor of Dionysius' theology is aesthetic: 'Denys can be regarded as the most aesthetic of all Christian theologians, because the aesthetic transcendence we know in this world (from the sensible as manifestation to the spiritual as what is manifest) provides the formal schema for understanding theological or mystical

transcendence (from the world to God)' " (McGinn, 161). This representation opposes standard distinctions of thought and experience, mind
and matter, allowing for the process of introspection itself to form the
subject of its own meditation, like the dreamer "writing the mystery of
himsel."

This Dionysian introspection filters through the early Middle Ages
to all mystical texts, most notably informing the intellectual structure
of Saint Bonaventure's *Itinerarum ad Mentis Deum*. In this treatise Bonaventure presents the contemplative mind's road to God. Bonaventure
traces our abilities to know and understand and offers steps to spiritual
enlightenment for the mystically inclined. He presents his discussion as
that of "the poor man in the desert," thus situating his meditation in a
line of descent from the earliest Christian sources, to whom the metaphor of spiritual aridity marks the beginning of understanding. After
first invoking the authority of Dionysius on the subject of the "trans-
ports of the soul," he turns to an investigation of the metaphorical steps
to God: "For we are so created that the material universe itself is a ladder by which we may ascend to God. And among things, some are ves-
tiges, others, images; some corporeal, others, spiritual: some temporal,
others everlasting" (Bonaventure, 200). He ascends Mount Alverno, to
venerate the stigmata received there by Saint Francis, in a type of Jacob's
ladder of spiritual knowing. The ladder follows the mind's itinerary
toward contemplative introversion and mystical apprehension and is
mirrored in Dionysian concepts of ascent and return. The ladder that
yields the sight of heaven is based on earth and that which it seeks to
overcome, material reality. The earthly grounding of the ladder becomes the perfect metaphor for the integrated relationship of the human mind, in spite of its spiritual yearnings, to the human body. To
Joyce's Finnegan who nightly falls off of his ladder into drunken sleep,
death, absence, and imaginative insight, the process of knowledge
nightly echoes "through deafths of durkness . . . a voice, the voce of
Shaun . . . voise from afar (and cert no purer puer palestrine e'er
chanted panangelical mid the clouds of Tu es Petrus . . .)" (*FW*, 407.11–
15). Shaun, Esau to Shem's Jacob in the oppositional world of the *Wake*,
sings the mysteries of the Mass, which reveal the hidden God of Moses'
cloudy revelation as the foundation of the Church and source of enlightenment.

The ladder shifts the cloudy obscurity of earthly perception to the
arena of the mind, "which is the image of God—an image which is
everlasting, spiritual, and within us" (Bonaventure, 39). In this inward
journey Bonaventure employs the primacy of the sense of sight to

mimic medieval patterns of intellection: corporeal, imaginative, and intellectual, with the last, contemplation, as the proper realm of reflection for spirituality. In this process of ascent and descent upon the ladder of knowing, "bodily senses inform the interior senses," and the visible world of recognition becomes the invisible world of faith in the absence of conceptualization. The process of apprehension lies in uniting the concrete and ineffable in the mind's inscription of God: "For every creature is by its very nature some kind of image and likeness of the eternal Wisdom, but especially one who, according to the Book of Scriptures, has been raised by the Spirit of Prophecy to prefigure spiritual things . . . that one which He willed to institute for signifying, and which has not only the character of sign in the ordinary sense of the term, but also the character of sacrament as well" (Bonaventure, 61). In this passage Bonaventure presents the Christocentric nature of images and likenesses as the key to understanding the relationship between the terms sign and sacrament, image and apprehension, language and created matter; it is transubstantive in nature. The ladder acts as a conductor of images so that "we are disposed to re-enter the mirror of our mind, wherein shine forth divine things" (Bonaventure, 61). And in the world of the *Wake*, we see ourselves pubwise "in his glass darkly" (*FW*, 355.9) to learn that "Wonderlawn's lost us for ever. Alis, alas, she broke the glass!" (*FW*, 270.20–22). Joyce's fall into the postlapserian imagination fuses sense and nonsense, reaching always to the clouds of Moses and many bushy, burning revelations in perfect fusion of mind and body.

Bonaventure's transition from earthly to divine understanding occurs only through the self-reflexive activity of the contemplative imagination and its counterpart in intellectual experience, the memory, which "retains the past by remembrance, the present by reception, and the future by foresight" (Bonaventure, 63). This action happens only at the behest of desire that seeks divine union. In this respect Bonaventure's three divisions of the intellect, "the generating mind, the word and love," which exist in the soul as "memory, intelligence and will consubstantial, co-equal and contemporary, and interpenetrating," reflect the theology of the incarnation as the investment in a single body of all the attributes of experience. In closing his meditation, Bonaventure restates the necessity of relinquishing all intellectual activities and attuning oneself to God, a process that is "most secret, which no one knows except him who desires it, and no one desires it except him who is penetrated to the marrow by the fire of the Holy Spirit" (Bonaventure, 99). At its conclusion the text enjoins the reader to "abandon the senses, intellectual activities," and most notably "visible and invisible things" in order to achieve the mystical sleep of the mind that allows one to "die into darkness." By integrating the Dionysian concept of darkness with the "supreme illumination of our mind" Bonaventure asserts the apophatic basis of his spiritual knowledge while still acknowledging that the inward mental journey arises from material understanding.

This death in darkness invokes the spiritual waking from the "sleep" of Songs 5:2. Richard Rolle's *Ego Dormio et Cor Meam Vigilat* articulates for mid-fourteenth century England this tradition present in Dionysius and Bonaventure and predominant in almost all mystical texts descriptive of the heart's wakening in sleep. Rolle enjoins the contemplative to "herken & here of luf" (Rolle, 50). His short work figures the soul's search for God in terms both amorous ("wha sall tyll my lemman say that for hys lufe me langes ay?") and pragmatic ("And tharfore all worldely solace the be-houes forsake . . . that thou may be in sylence") (Rolle, 59). Rolle's text retains Dionysius' investment in silence and Bonaventure's steps to God, and in turn would influence John of the Cross's celebration of amatory spirituality (Benedictine, 75). In *Finnegans Wake* Rolle contributes to the speaker of "my heart, my coming forth of darkness" (*FW*, 493.34), a type of Joyce's ideal insomniac who "fell with a roll and a rumble" (*FW*, 45.02) down Dionysius' "*Ecclesiastical and Celestial Hierarchies. The Ascending. The Descending*" through "*Ambages and Their Role*" (*FW*, 298). McHugh glosses "ambages" as "dark language for deceit and concealment"—a handy circumlocution for divine names and other tantalizingly appropriate obscurities. The *Wake*'s hidden mysteries of God, sex, sin, and grace converge by night in which, one way or another, "the soul of everyelsebody rolled into its olesoleself" (*FW*, 329.18) literally raises the dead "as merrily as we rolled along . . . as if to pass away in a cloud" (*FW*, 615.21). Consummately ascended, the dreaming mind is free to "roll away the reel world" (*FW*, 64.25) in order to take up superior things: "And I suppose they told you too that my roll of life is not natural?" (*FW*, 149.14). Against nature, perhaps, the celestial hierarchies of hidden things dominate the dark "where their role was to rule the round roll that Rollo and Rullo rolled round. Those were the grandest gynecollege histories . . . in the Janesdanes Lady Andersdaughter Universary" (*FW*, 389.8–11). The universal mind peruses "mid shadowed landscape" the union of form, "gynecollege" or otherwise, with ineffability in the representation of the world by night. Better than "Boccuccia's Enameron" the dark language of concealment reveals word into form, sight into mind, and world into being: "behold, she had instantt with her handmade as to graps the myth in mid the air. I will to show herword in flesh." The mystical enunciation prods the dreaming mind toward the dawn of all stories, writing, and creativity from sleep: "Approach not for ghost sake! It is dormition!" (*FW,* 561.24–28). The *Wake*'s somniloquence announces, "self exiled in upon his own ego," the "heartsoul dormant" in suspended attention to life and death.

By what further itinerary does this Wakeful sleep find its road to art? Dionysius' negative tradition and Bonaventure's intellectual apprehension shape the anonymous *Cloud of Unknowing,* fourteenth-century England's response to the negative way. In turn, the *Cloud* shapes John of the Cross's *Dark Night of the Soul.* Humble and homely instructions for contemplation belie the *Cloud*'s sophisticated consciousness of itself as a form of psychology. The *Cloud* author abandons any conscious means of divine knowing by instead releasing all sense of authority or control "acordyng wil vnto God" (*Cloud,* 92). In the course of his instruction for the devout, the *Cloud* author establishes the value of spiritual darkness and introspection to the process of cognition, and thus refines the distinction between an essentially mental experience of divinity and the products of the faculty of the imagination. The work then follows Dionysius and Bonaventure by linking body and mind in spite of their apparent opposition.

The central metaphors of the text derive from Dionysius and express the nature of contemplation as a dissolution into darkness and the "cloude of forgetyng."[1] The nature of the dark provides the context for reading the book: "For when I sey derknes, I mene a lackyng of knowyng; as alle that thing that thou knowest not, or elles that thou hast forgetyn, it is derk to thee, for thou seest it not with thi goostly iye. And for this skile it is not clepid a cloude of the eire, bot a cloude of vnknowyng that is bitwin thee & thi God" (*Cloud,* 23). The work of contemplation involves relinquishing concepts of time and space, and instead living in a suspended present that is the "derk" of the "goostly iye" (*Cloud,* 52–53). The cognitive abandon of discursive reason for nothingness consumes the mind so that "when it is betyng upon this derke cloude of vnknowyng, alle other images [are] put doun and for geten" (*Cloud,* 58). This forgetting, enabled by radical self-awareness, frees the mind of images and ideas and prepares for introspective enlightenment.

In his spiritual guidance the *Cloud* author asserts the power of forgetting against memory's mental clutter: "For why mynde or thinkyng of any creature that euer God maad, or of any of theire dedes outher, it is a maner of goostly light; for the iye of thi soule is openid on it & euen ficchid ther-apon, as the iye of a schoter is apon the prich that he schote"

(*Cloud*, 24). This focused view of God results from the failure of thought and discourse, and remains possible so long as the intellect desires only an integrated fusion with darkness. The mental discipline required to maintain this focus fails under too literal a meditation upon Christ, which inevitably leads to less profound speculation until finally, before you know it, "thou schalt be scaterid" (*Cloud*, 27). This mental scattering, or distraction, mimics the pattern and spirit of the Fall and finds its restitution only in the spiritual ascesis of forgetting. As a property of imagination and feeling that lives in the material and presides in the senses, memory remains one of the first and most untrustworthy of mental functions to the *Cloud* author. The "scateryng" of recollection may descend into more pointed and sensual reflections: "For whith a nakyd sodein thought of any of hem presing agens thio wile & thi wetyng, of alit be no sinne aretted vnto thee—for it is the pyne of the original sinne presing agens thi power" (*Cloud*, 35). The point of the stirrings of memory is clear: to recollect is human, to forget, divine. To the end of forgetting, the author advocates specific techniques of mental discipline. When faced with the memory of sin or temptation the author advises: "to couer hem with a thicke cloude of forgetyng, as thei neuer had ben done in this liif of thee, ne of other man outher. & if thei ofte rise, ofte put theim doun; &, schortly to sey, as ofte as thei rise, as ofte put theim doun" (*Cloud*, 66). Forgetting becomes a willful act of repression whose necessity suggests the omnipresence of sin and distraction, in the fourteenth-century contemplative world and the twentieth-century Wakean consciousness whose slips of "m'm'ry" (*FW*, 460.20) intangibly reveal the presence of guilt and sin.

A similar "forgetting" must exist on the level of bodily sensation and expression; however, the intellectual and material, despite their essential division, unite in metaphors from the sensual world. The *Cloud* author gives the example of "steryng." This stirring, like other manifestations of enthusiasm, must be measured "by desires, & not by pases of feet" (*Cloud*, 112) in order to measure inner alertness. The relationship of matter to spirit correlates internal and external attention. The contemplative thus regards his inward and outward meditation in the following way: "For what tyme that a soule dispose him effectuely to this werk, than as fast sodenly—vnwetyng him-self at worche—the body, at arauenture bifore er he bygan was sumwhat heeldyng downwards on o syde or on other for these of the flesche, by vertue of the spirit schal set it upright, folowyng in maner & in licnes bodely the werk of the spirit that is maad gosstly & thus it is moste semely to be" (*Cloud*,

113). Physical stirring thus correlates with the insurrection of the mind, to the *Cloud* author's greater discontent. False inspiration and dubious sensory experience, not only in the *Cloud* but also generally in medieval accounts of visionary states and spiritual ecstasy, inspire doubt regarding the authenticity and authority of experience. The failure to control memory and desire against uncertainty characterizes the basic state of human consciousness—how does one sort high revelation from the merely fantastic? How does one know, with certainty, anything whatsoever? For the *Cloud* author artistic production springs particularly from these questions of the visual imagination. The devil forges images that "enflaume so the ymaginacion of his contemplatiyues withe the fire of helle, that sodenly, withoutyn discrecion, thei schete oute theire corius conceites" (*Cloud,* 103). Scattering, experience, descent into personality, and lapse into subjectivity at once oppose and link art and spirituality. Phantasms, devils, genuine apparitions, and ecstasy beyond the senses directly proceed from human, sensorial, material bases of knowledge and yet by necessity reconstruct Joyce's twentieth-century "real Absence" of "m'm'ry" and other lapses.

In order to illustrate this connection of body to mind, imagination to spirit, the *Cloud* author sketches out his mental concept of ideas and images. Before describing the design of the mind he warns of the error of too literal an understanding of language, which would impede the more important spiritual message. He identifies language as part of the realm of matter because "al it be spokyn in bodely wordes" (*Cloud,* 114); however, he divides experience in such a way that he understands the mind according to the distinctions of "reson & wille" against the power of "ymaginacion & sensualite" (*Cloud,* 115). In this mental hierarchy the faculties have the task of sorting out sensory information from the internal and external world. In his description of the hierarchy of the mind the *Cloud* author essentially follows Aquinas, who further understands the imagination to accommodate common sense, imagination, opinion, and memory. In affirming the senses as the portals of the soul, Aquinas observes that the apprehension presupposes a meeting place for sensation and that "the faculty of opinion corresponds to a definite need of our animal organism" (Bundy, 217). Against apophatic mysticism's denial of the body's significance, this assertion of the "animal organism" reenforces the distinction of sense and intellect and suggests that, try as one might, in human nature sensory experience will prevail.

Aquinas further states that "the soul understands nothing without a phantasm," bound, of course, by the corporeal structures of the senses

(Bundy, 219). In other words, Aquinas suggests, following Aristotle, that all knowledge must proceed from an empirical basis and therefore naturally requires the senses. To figure the incorporeal, the imagination must construct its own "phantasm," or form of mental representation, despite the imagination's inability to transcend time and space. Through these concepts Aquinas presents the crux of negative theology's relationship with the imagination, especially that produced by the most privileged of senses, vision. To Dionysius the object of contemplation must be mystical cognition; to Aquinas, the object of contemplation cannot be anything but that which the senses mediate, cognition per se. In each instance the goal is contemplation, although differently defined. In both the Dionysian and the Thomistic conceptualizations of the mind, the clearest distrust lies with the products of the imagination—suspect to one system because they are given a palpable shape, suspect to the other system because they are not concrete enough. This distrust creates an anxiety about artistic creation and raises questions about the mind's uneasy ability to represent the function of the world within or outside of itself. To return to the *Cloud* and its admonitions to "forget" or "put under a cloud of unknowing" the stimulation of the senses and their accompanying mental distraction, the author gives practical advice not only to the mystic in search of divine union, but also, unwittingly, to the artist in need of aesthetic inspiration. In this connection Maimonides, one of the greatest interpreters of Aristotle to the Middle Ages, suggests that the best part of the imagination emerges when "the senses are at rest; then divine inspiration is possible, both in dreams and in prophecy (Bundy, 214). Bundy quotes Maimonides: " 'The imaginative faculty,' he explains, 'acquires such an efficiency in its action that it sees the thing as if it came from without, and perceives it as if through the medium of bodily senses' . . . That which has our attention in waking experience becomes the subject of imagination in sleep" (Bundy, 214). The sleep of the mind allows for the introspection of perception to awaken into the "cloud Incertitude" (*FW*, 178.31) of the negative tradition and all those who nightly rest "Head-in-Clouds" (*FW*, 18.23).

Thus far the mystical aesthetics presented by Dionysius, Bonaventure, and the *Cloud* author assign a positive and necessary value to the state of unknowing and its visual correlative of darkness. Despite their seeming opposition to the status of the imagination, they nonetheless rely upon products of its manufacture for their conceptualization of everything, including nothingness. In this respect the texts of mysticism serve as theoretical models for the impulse toward creativity, representation, and the limits and possibilities of human understanding. To explore and potentially to resolve their own inherent contradictions the mystical texts return to the theology of the incarnation. Joyce, for his part, is enabled by the mystics' sorting out of knowledge and perception to construct his central metaphors of the nature of inquiry and its relationship to the body, presented in the evolution of consciousness from *Portrait* through *Finnegans Wake*.

However, it is John of the Cross in *The Ascent of Mount Carmel* and *The Dark Night of the Soul* who contributes to the study of mysticism the most detailed exegesis of the nature of the night and role of the mind in the eroticism of approaching God. *The Dark Night of the Soul*, which Joyce said "cries and faints with such ecstatic passion," the image of the crucifixion and the schematic drawing of ascent that accompanies that treatise, show John of the Cross to be for Joyce the ideal contemplative figure, in whom sexuality, artistry, spirituality, and the potential for reordered epistemology powerfully converge. In the fall and redemption of *Finnegans Wake* Joyce presents the essence of John of the Cross's investigation of the ontology of the dark, the purgation of the faculties, and the mechanisms of comprehension, and by so doing establishes his "will to show herword in flesh" and thereby subvert ordinary thought.

John of the Cross stands at the lattermost end of the medieval mystical tradition inaugurated by Dionysius the Areopagite. Writing in sixteenth-century Spain, he benefits from the spiritual tradition of Bonaventure and the *Cloud* author, as well as from the affective theology of Theresa of Avila, his mentor in the Carmelite order (Louth, 180). Like that of Bonaventure, the theology of John of the Cross is absorbed in the process of divine love. He meticulously traces the contemplative forgetting of the sensual world for the spiritual agonies and rewards of obscurity. John of the Cross was extremely popular among his followers, especially young women entering the Carmelite life. His spiritual masterwork is *The Ascent of Mount Carmel*, which divides into three parts: the *Ascent*, which outlines the necessity of purgation on the path to God; the poem entitled *The Dark Night* and its accompanying explication, *The Dark Night of the Soul*; and the sketch of the ascent of the mount, which sets forth visually a diagram of contemplation. Elizabeth Wilhelmsen asserts that the saint possessed an artistic temperament that motivated him to write about "esthetic and discursive cognitive activity" as a means of spiritual discourse (Wilhelmsen, 33). Although she works hard to separate the mystical and poetic act, she demonstrates that the texts strive to perceive spirituality in aesthetic terms. Joyce names the work as a major source for the "treatment of the night,"

and the poem, its explication, and his drawings suggestively fore-
shadow much Joycean darkness and unknowing.

A brief account of the poem *The Dark Night* can establish its relationship to devotional and erotic literature. The tradition of spiritual love
poetry derives from the Song of Songs, which, in turn, emerges from
ancient Egyptian secular love poetry. John of the Cross's poem contains
eight stanzas inaugurated "by the path of spiritual negation." The
poem begins "En una noche oscura"—on a dark night, and describes
a lover's meeting. The soul, figured as an impassioned woman, leaves
the house in the still of night by means of a secret ladder in order to
meet her lover. She slips unseen in darkness to their meeting place and
praises the virtues of the night that guides her, better than the light of
dawn, to the moment of union: "Amado con amada / amada en el
Amado transformada"—"the Lover with his beloved / transforming
the beloved in her Lover." This is the essence of infused contemplation;
the soul achieves rapport with God in human terms likened only to
sexual union. The poem concludes with three stanzas of voluptuous
sensuality. In the first the lover sleeps upon the breast of the woman
while she caresses him in the breeze. This same breeze in the next
stanza "wound[s]" her neck with a "gentle hand / suspending all [her]
senses." This wound so arouses that the senses, stimulated and soothed,
leave off feeling altogether, and the soul, in the final stanza, abandons
her sense of self and all things, leaving her cares "forgotten among the
lilies." The poem ends with the relinquishing of all sensation and perception in the ultimate pleasure of the Lover. As theology the poem
explores the importance of escape, darkness, secrecy, and self-abandon
as the road to God. As art it overwhelmingly relies upon the realm of
the senses as metaphor and meaning of union with God.[2]

The Dark Night of the Soul explicates the spiritual significance of the
poem by devoting a chapter of meditation and interpretation to each
line of the poetry. The work is incomplete, stopping at the end the second stanza, after the soul leaves the house by the ladder and proceeds
to the "glad night" of stanza 3. By editorial tradition the commentary
divides into two parts: the night of the sense and the night of the spirit.
The night of the sense, which occupies half of the exposition, emerges
from commentary upon the first three lines of stanza 1 and concludes
with the house at rest in the night as the departing image for the world
of sense. Both the night of the sense and the night of the spirit explore
the Dionysian concepts of darkness and secrecy to which the soul must
attain in order to achieve illumination. The dark night of the soul, while
potentially harrowing in its insistence upon loss of self, in fact comes to

be a positive state for the contemplative. The first book, that of sense, begins by establishing sensuality and pleasure, or most sensory experience, as "all the passions and desires with respect to their mischievous desires and motions."[3] The work begins with an exposition upon the seven deadly sins as they pertain to the novice contemplative who is earnest, to a fault, in the life of prayer. The state of sin necessitates the "dark night." The night "which . . . is contemplation" produces its own kind of "darkness or purgation, corresponding to the two parts of man's nature—namely the sensual and the spiritual" (Peers, 61). The night of the sense is common, according to John of the Cross, while the cleansing night of the spirit comes to only the spiritually proficient.

Although the commentary expounds upon sin, its goal is sensual purgation, in which "the road to . . . perception and vision of the virtue of God" lies in "being unable to form any conception of God or to walk by meditation produced by imaginary consideration" (Peers, 81). This is the ideal state of apophatic mysticism in which the loss of the imaginative faculties permits "secret, peaceful and loving infusion from God," which renders the soul, in the words of the poem, "Kindled in love with yearnings." One achieves this state of emptiness by overcoming the limitations of the body. During the night of the sense darkness begins as the contemplative feels the call to devotion, usually signified by the purgation of sensual desire, the loss of memory other than thoughts of God, and the emptying of the imagination. This purgation, however, is described in terms of bodily pleasure and desire. Early in its discussion of the night of the sense the work comments upon the "imperfections" of the body during prayer. Echoing perhaps the *Cloud of Unknowing,* and certainly honoring a traditional concern of monastic worshipers, John of the Cross provides guidance for those who experience sexual arousal during prayer: "For often it comes to pass that, in their very spiritual exercises, when they are powerless to prevent it, there arise and assert themselves in the sensual part of the soul impure acts and motions, and sometimes this happens even when the spirit is deep in prayer, or engaged in the Sacrament of Penance or in the Eucharist" (Peers, 47). The saint explains that the source of arousal may be love of God, inspiration from the devil, or fear of one's own sexual desires. Regardless of cause John of the Cross counsels believers to direct their attention to the absence of delight and the removal of stimulating mental images in order that the "angel of Satan . . . the spirit of fornication" may not assault "with vile considerations and representations which are most visible to the imagination" (Peers, 88). Even in this night body and mind remain intimately linked.

The discussion of the night of the sense continues its exploration of the real presence of the body amidst the glorification of absence through imagery of nurturing. In the book of sense, John of the Cross repeatedly figures the soul as a child nursing at the breast of God: "the soul . . . spiritually nurtured and caressed by God, even as is the tender child by its loving mother, who warms it with the heat of her bosom" (Peers, 38). The simile becomes metaphor slightly later in the book, when God quite literally weans away the spiritually mature and makes them eat "the food of robust persons . . . infused contemplation," which consists in "the knowledge of oneself and of one's misery" (Peers, 76). Elsewhere the act of receiving excessive communion, eating God too often, signifies wrongful indulgence, a kind of spiritual gluttony. The night of the sense prevents infantile cravings by "drying up" the "breasts of sensuality" so that "there remains nothing in that aridity and detachment save the yearning to serve God" (Peers, 86). As befits the book of spirit, breast and nurturing imagery largely disappear, with the most notable exception of a reference to Song of Songs 8 : 1 in which the Bride desires to kiss her brother who is nursed at her mother's breasts. The imagery of eating and nursing supplants infantile eroticism with the desire to fall into the passive knowledge of God: "neither is their preparation [for union with God] in attachment to the breast of delectable meditations, belonging to the faculties of sense, which gave the soul pleasure; such preparation consists rather in the lack of the one and withdrawal from the other" (Peers, 80). Instead, the "road to his conception and vision" consists in leaving off direct nurture and "being unable to form any conception of God" (Peers, 81). The absence of pleasure, stimulation, and imaginative capacity put the house to rest and permit the egress into the night of the mind.

This exit leads out of the house and into the darkness of the night of the spirit. The goal in this book, "pleasure in nothing," emerges from "emptiness, darkness and obscurity" (Peers, 119) as the mental correlative of perceptual and cognitive abandonment. This second half of the book redefines darkness as "infused contemplation," or, following Dionysius' "mystical theology," a state that produces union and "affliction and torment." The night of the spirit assumes that imagination, memory, and cognition are in check and begins the real work of ascent and descent "in darkness and secure. By the secret ladder." The darkness leads to a nothingness made profound not merely by the absence of the senses, purged in the night of the sense, but by dwelling in "emptiness, darkness and obscurity" according to the words of Paul: *nihil habentes, et omnia possidentes* (Peers, 119). In desiring no desire, knowledge of God is like falling "deeply and passionately in love" (Peers, 132). For this knowledge, which is the essence of desire, the most apt metaphor is that of sleep, for "it is needful for the enamoured soul, in order to attain its desired end . . . going forth at night, when all the domestics in its house are sleeping and at rest—that is, when the low operations, passions and desires of the soul (who are the people of the household) are, because it is night, sleeping and at rest" (Peers, 147). In the putting to sleep of the house of the mind and the body, the exposition of negation reaches its culmination, repeating not only its premises but those of the tradition from which it emerges. To explicate the nature of sleep, how "through darkness, the soul walks securely," John of the Cross writes that "the sensual desires are put to sleep and mortified . . . all the faculties are void and useless; and in addition to all this a thick and heavy cloud is upon the soul" (Peers, 150). The soul emerges from the house into nonrepresentation and the analogy of sleep, like lovemaking, holds the most potent human equivalent for the unconscious descent into the nature of desire.

In the sleep of darkness the soul leaves the house by means of "a very secret ladder . . . the which ladder . . . is living faith" (Peers, 149). In keeping with its tradition this ladder rests in the world of sense and thought, but lifts upward to the realm of the nonconceptual. The ladder leads to knowledge through other metaphors of understanding, especially that of fire and its origin in Moses' encounter with the burning bush. The climactic image of fire in the night of the spirit becomes an image of self-consuming ecstasy. On the highest rung of the ladder of ascent, "the soul continues to rise above all things and above itself, and to mount upward to God. For love is like fire, which ever rises upward with the desire to be absorbed in the centre of its sphere" (Peers, 75). For John of the Cross the nature of desire, and of reality itself, circles back to a distinction between being and nonbeing, diffusion and integration, and his fiery construction of identity, divine or otherwise, predicates itself on absence and lack.

The fires of passion and mystery kindle equally the enlightened understanding of the night of the spirit. John of the Cross insists that the will and the imagination produce the paired afflictions of uncertainty and memory, and that these are the true sufferings of the night of the soul. Once again, the nature of proper understanding emerges only after one has relinquished the things of the world and entered "secret wisdom." No one but God follows this private concept, and the mind "cannot account for it or imagine it." In this respect Moses at the burning bush becomes the model for understanding and revelation, for not even "with the interior imagination did he dare to meditate, for it seemed to him that his imagination was very far away and was too dumb, not only to express any part of that which he understood concerning God, but even to have the capacity to receive aught therefrom" (Peers, 160). In his exposition John of the Cross once again follows the tradition of Dionysius, who ensured the popularity of the motif of the burning bush in the West by reiterating the inability of language to mime with precision the operations of consciousness. As John of the Cross states, the meaning of secrecy inheres in this limitation of the representing mind: "And thus, when by means of this illumination the soul discerns this truth, namely, that it cannot reach it, still less explain it, by common or human language, it rightly calls it secret" (Peers, 162). The images of the burning bush and the ladder of faith coalesce in the sleeping mind of Jacob, who, like Tim Finnegan, envisions the "ladder of contemplation . . . whereon angels were ascending and descending, from God to men, and from man to God . . . All this took place by night, when Jacob slept, in order to express how secret is this road and ascent . . . and how different from that of man's knowledge . . . namely, to be ever losing oneself and becoming as nothing" (Peers, 166). To become as nothing, to simultaneously seek and abandon the search for self-disclosure in the sleep of the mind, comprises the essence of *The Dark Night of the Soul* and is the artistic basis of Joyce's search for a language with which to express subjectivity. The manuscript ends shortly after describing the self-consuming fire of love that the night of the spirit induces. Scholars originally assumed that John of the Cross died before its completion, but later research has demonstrated that he lived for many years after abandoning it.[4] While his reasons for doing so remain speculative, the unfinished work suggests an artifact that, by its own logic, ceases to exist. After all, the theology that produces the self-consuming fire of love disbelieves in the power of words. But John of the Cross did attempt to surmount the limitations of language by restructuring its presentation both in his drawing of the crucifixion and later in his sketch of the ascent of the mount, which provides a visual demonstration of falling asleep and forgetting the senses among the lilies of his poem.

John of the Cross's drawing awakens the relationship between mysticism, visuality, and art. His depiction of the crucifixion (figure 1) precedes the composition of *The Dark Night* and its commentary and powerfully suggests the aesthetic issues present in that later poetry. The drawing represents a vision revealed during prayer, problematic for the

Figure 1. Christ Crucified, a drawing by Saint John of the Cross

saint who distrusted such images. Viewed from above, Christ's head is
bent and the sinewy body drapes to earth. The angle hides the face and
diminishes the significance of the body in favor of the limpness of
death. This rendering points downward to earth and to mortality, not
only of Christ but of all fleshly things. But the extremely unusual perspective reveals the saint's radical meditation upon the relation of the
viewer to vision, to art, to God, and to the self-effacement at the heart
of John of the Cross's own writing: in the words of the *Wake*, his own
"cruelfiction."

In this image the human potential of Christ is diminished, already
unusual in that the crucifixion is the most mundane sacrifice. The body
recedes to earth, yet in the ultimate fulfillment of Jacob's ladder moves
upward to the clouds. The hidden face conceals not only the human
pain and death central to the idea of the crucifixion but also its promise
of divine redemption. Whether this is the shell of the resurrected Christ
or an image of forsaken man becomes, quite literally, a matter of perspective. The image holds tremendous potential for either reading and
as such questions the ability of the human mind and eye to make distinctions of time and space, of life and death. Without the evidence of
the empty tomb, the instability of vision and the potential of Christ's
"Real Absence" (*FW*, 536.05) become the most compelling and present
of subjects. The identity of the viewer is equally perplexing because the
perspective eliminates any ordinary sight. The meditation thus encompasses speculation not only about the risen Christ but also about the
imagination, capable of expressing absence and incertitude. The relation of body to mind, of art to interpretation lies in the uncertain visual
domain. In this respect this image anticipates the value of the negative
at the center of John of the Cross's poetic corpus and his sketch of
Mount Carmel, which situates the very idea of God between annihilation and creativity.

The twentieth-century response to John of the Cross clarifies his importance theologically and artistically. In 1926 Pius XI declared him
doctor of mystical theology. His later biographer, Bruno de Jesus-Marie,
discussed the image of the crucifixion with José Maria Sert and Salvador Dali, who painted *The Christ of St. John of the Cross* in response to
the drawing's startling perspective. The editors of the more recent collected works of the saint note the remarks of René Huyghe, former
conservator-in-chief of the Louvre, on the subject of the drawing: "Saint
John of the Cross escapes right out of those visual habits by which all
artists form a part of their period. He knows nothing of the rules and

limitations of contemporary vision; he is not dependent on the manner of seeing current in his century; he is dependent on nothing but the object of his contemplation . . . The vertical perspective—bold, almost violent, emphasized by light and shade—in which he caught his Christ on the cross cannot be matched in contemporary art; in the context of that art it is hardly imaginable" (*Collected Works*, 38).

Equally radical is the value of that perspective to the alternative strategies of visual and verbal representation in the sketch of the ascent of Mount Carmel (figure 2), whose abstraction reinforces the conceptual negation present in the saint's literature. The sketch, drawn in 1579, is the only surviving example of John of the Cross's habit of presenting his thought in a visual form for the education of the novices. The arrangement of words on the page, as well as their meaning, repeats the saint's goal of apophatic knowledge. Simultaneously resisting and absorbing ordinary gender distinctions, the sketch presents a highly eroticized conceptualization of darkness, nothingness, and nowhere, whose center and sphere both delimit and dissolve any sense of boundary or space. As such, it perfectly represents the aesthetic possibilities inherent within its own mystical premises, and serves as a marvelous template for the diagram at the center of the "Night Lessons" chapter of *Finnegans Wake*, meant to enlighten the children, novices of another kind (figure 3).

The ascent of the mount begins with a series of admonitions written vertically at the bottom of the page, which urge the contemplative to renounce all earthly satisfaction by desiring its opposite, or by relinquishing any impulse toward desire whatsoever. This basis in desire serves the image well; the center shaft extends along the path of the perfect spirit and seeks "nothing" repeatedly, to find that at its summit, the top of the mount, there is nothing. The upward and downward movement of Jacob's ladder is captured by the rooting of the image in earthly desire and pleasure, as well as by the inscriptions along either side of the shaft of the sketch, which write upward and downward of the rejection of spiritual and material things, and the side message, which reads "Now that I least desire them," suggesting the measure by which they may be quantified. The left side of the diagram progresses down the spiritual ladder by writing upside down the heavenly possessions that the contemplative must reject in order to reach the summit of the mount. These heavenly rewards are measured by time—"now that I no longer desire them"—and taken in conjunction with the goods of the earth outlined on the opposite side suggest that the abandonment

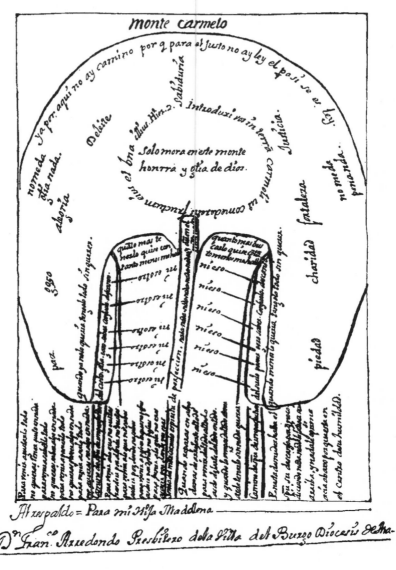

Figure 2a. Sketch of Mount Carmel by Saint John of the Cross

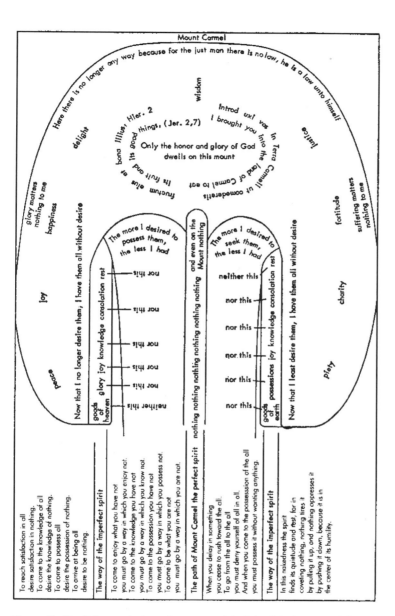

Figure 2b. English translation of terms used in Saint John's original drawing

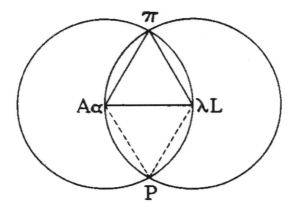

Figure 3. Diagram at the center of the "Night Lessons" chapter of *Finnegans Wake*

of desire through suppression of consciousness and the senses renders time and space more relative than ever.

The darkness of the night, the summit of the mount, and the sleep of sensibility coalesce along the central axis, the way of the "perfect spirit." This way leads to nothing, and this nada quite literally points not only to the climax of the negative mystical experience, but also to the visual center of consciousness, which is no consciousness. At the top of the mount nothing is also God, and the quote from Jeremiah 2:7, "I brought you into the land of Carmel to eat its fruit and its good things," surrounds this nothingness, darkness, and obscurity with sensuality. The top of the sketch says that experience has a limitation because it is self-referential: "Here there is no longer any way because for the just man there is no law, he is a law unto himself." However, the involuted logic of the diagram and its rootedness in the nature of desire itself suggest that knowledge emerges from a combination of past and present memory, experience and descent into humility, all of which occurs in a circulatory manner. The outlines of the sketch itself suggest this organic representation. Resembling simultaneously the brain seated upon the spine, the penis, an image of sexual intercourse, or perhaps an open womb, the drawing blurs distinctions of physical and mental being. In *The Dark Night of the Soul* John of the Cross figures the soul as both female and male, and the divine consummation suggested by the "desire to be absorbed in the centre of its sphere" at the top of the ladder certainly ignores any idea of sexual orientation, expressing only an impulse toward enfolding. The eroticism of the drawing is inherent in the premise of cognitive abandonment and release of identity that lies at the core of negative mysticism. In the *Wake* the saint preaches to the young novices with "his jewelled pederect to the allmystry cielung" (*FW*, 155.23), pointing out how John of the Cross's sexual metaphor constructs a representation of consciousness that reaches beyond the verbal and, by the power of its sensual philosophy, allows for the making of art.

This sensual knowing lies at the root of Joyce's fascination with the texts of the apophatic mystical tradition. He reaches to this tradition to understand the origin of images in body and mind and in words on the page, and the fundamental interdependence of these origins. In so doing he redefines the nature of perception as an intellectual phenomenon that reflects the union of the mind and the body, linked by the strandentwining cable of all words to the flesh of the medieval contemplative tradition. John of the Cross's "footwear for the poor discalced" (*FW*, 448.30) gracefully trods the mind's road to aesthetic cognition. He buries "m'm'ry" and understanding under the "cloud Incertitude" (*FW*, 178.31) in his quest for self-disclosure, forgotten among the lilies, in the sensual sleep of the mind. His itinerary leads Joyce and all those who would think upon things "supernocturnal" (*FW*, 398.17) to "walk while ye have the night" (*FW*, 473.22), so the day may never come wherein no one shall wake.

2

Against Actuality
Critical Writings in Context

To read Joyce's critical writings in the context of their late Victorian intellectual milieu allows one "to conclude purely negatively from the positive absence" (*FW*, 108.24) that Joyce looked to mystical literature in order to put ideas and images into words. Joyce's early works inherit the traditions of those Victorian writers whose theory of art consciously derived from mystical literature's philosophical concern with the sensual and the subjective. Joyce's critical writings demonstrate his opinion of medieval mystical literature and its particular significance to Irish consciousness and art. The writings emerge from a larger intellectual context shaped by four separate yet related strains of Victorian aesthetics—Walter Pater's subjectivity, Francis Thompson's religious faith, James Thomson's urban nihilism, and Gerard Manley Hopkins' visual theology of perception—all of which acknowledge the relative status of the senses in the construction of memory, absence, and understanding and suggest a unified concept of sensation and cognition, body and mind.[1]

Joyce was not alone in his efforts to articulate the theology of Irish aesthetics. Yeats's prose also points to the late Victorian interest in medieval heritage, history, and hermeneutics as an incipient form of modernist self-expression. His writing encapsulates the concept of secular religiosity expressed through the medium of culture, myth, and national identity. In "The Celtic Element in Literature," Yeats argues that the "imagination" of the late nineteenth century is "as ready as it was at the coming of the tales of Arthur and of the Grail for a new intoxication. The reaction against the rationalism of the eighteenth century has mingled with a reaction against the materialism of the nineteenth century . . . The arts by brooding upon their own intensity have become religious, and are seeking . . . to write a sacred book" (Yeats, 187). Writing in 1897, Yeats locates in aestheticism and decadence the intellectual antecedents of nineteenth-century medievalism and the forebears of twentieth-century introspective literature. In reaction to the forces of rationalism and materialism this literature developed a kind of meditative practice whose "brooding" habits of mind produced a century of artistic navel gazing and preoccupation with uncertainty and perception. Yeats's statement suggests that the contemplative activities of the late Victorian mind, nurtured by an intellectual and theological identification with the Middle Ages, generated an artistic impulse that provided the basis for an antirational, antibourgeois ideology. This impulse matches the religious and political insubordination that Joyce champions in Blake, and both Yeats's and Joyce's vision emerge from a common association of medieval literature, cultural rebellion, and spiritual consciousness. Yeats identifies in the literature of his contemporaries a deliberate (and cyclic) reappropriation of the past in the writing of the present that results in the creation of "a sacred book."

In "The Autumn of the Body" Yeats pursues the sacred text of modernist culture by identifying ineffability and unknowability as concepts that must exist in order to inaugurate a literature of the interior life. The opening lines are Paterian not only in tone, but also in content: "Our thoughts and emotions are often but spray flung up from hidden tides that follow a moon no eye can see" (Yeats, 189). The "spiritual and unemphatic" qualities that Yeats describes exist in order to fulfill his aesthetic criteria, and they demand "decadence . . . [defined as the] many things which positive science, the interpreter of exterior law, has always denied: communion of mind in thought and without words, foreknowledge in dreams and in visions, and the coming among us of the dead, and of much else." Although Yeats does not here directly address the traditions of medieval mystical practice, he nonetheless invokes the same resistance to science and reason through faith in absence, insubstantiality, and death. Yeats's essay focuses on the proposition that "we know nothing but the fading and flowering of the world" (Yeats, 192) and that the weight of meaning and expression, because it cannot be carried by traditional institutions or conventional ontology, will fall to the arts who are "to take upon their shoulders the burdens that have fallen from the shoulders of the priests" (Yeats, 193). The sacred book craved by the collective late-nineteenth-century consciousness emerges from a theological sensibility that understands literary expression as a secular "revelation of the mind to itself."[2]

Like Yeats in his attempt to characterize the temperament of Celtic literature past and present, Joyce in "Ireland, Isle of Saints and Sages" locates the origins of Irish culture in the monastic history of the Middle Ages. He begins the article by proclaiming that "nations have their ego" and, true to his metaphor, psychoanalyzes the national mentality that made possible Ireland's profound influence on the establishment of monasteries at home and abroad, and its central role in the proliferation of learning and culture. He locates the "roots of the Irish temperament" quite pointedly in the Middle Ages and implies that one must comprehend Ireland's medieval heritage, which overwhelmingly formed (and continues to inform) its culture, in order to understand its current psychology. As he says to the Italian audience whom he addresses, "Ireland at the time was an immense seminary . . . it is more than likely (in view of the religious fervour that still prevails in Ireland, of which you, nourished on the food of skepticism in recent years, can hardly form a correct idea) that this glorious past is not a fiction based on the spirit of self-glorification" (*CW*, 155). Joyce asserts that his argument rests on a realistic rather than fanciful notion of the medieval foundation of Ireland's religious and cultural present.

He argues for the profound importance of medieval culture by considering the effect of Dionysius the Areopagite on European history and reclaiming his ninth-century translation by John Scotus Erigena as further evidence of Ireland's intellectual greatness. Joyce remarks the massive cultural, aesthetic, intellectual, and religious influence of the monastic Dionysius directly, as well as by associating him with other figures. As Ellmann notes, Joyce confuses Dionysius the pseudo-Areopagite with Dionysius the Areopagite of Athens, and Saint Denis of Paris. The logic and syntax of the passage suggest that Joyce also appropriates for Ireland Duns Scotus, a Scot, whom he conflates with the Irish-born Scotus Erigena. Joyce states that "Ireland had the honour of producing the three great heresiarchs John Duns Scotus, Macarius and Vergilius Solivagus." Joyce states that Scotus Erigena, "a mystical pantheist," translated from the Greek "the books of mystical theology of Dionysius, the pseude-Areopagite, patron saint of the French nation. This presented to Europe for the first time the transcendental philosophy of the Orient, which had as much influence on the course of European religious thought as later the translations of Plato, made in the time of Pico della Mirandola, had on the development of the profane Italian civilization. It goes without saying that such an innovation (which seemed like a lifegiving breath resurrecting the dead bones of orthodox theology piled up in an inviolable churchyard, a field of Ardath) did not have the sanction of the Pope, who invited Charles the Bald to send both the book and the author to Rome under escort, probably because he wanted them both to taste the delights of papal courtesy" (CW, 160). While Joyce correctly attributes the translation of Dionysius to the ninth-century Scotus Erigena, whose name means "originating from Erin," the structure and progression of the argument that follows imply that he and the thirteenth-century theologian Duns Scotus, with whom Hopkins is associated, are one. Notably, and rightly, Joyce comments upon the power of Dionysian mysticism to invigorate theology with alternative configurations of knowledge, and his argument would credit medieval Ireland for its dissemination. Indeed, in a lecture dedicated to enumerating the achievements of early Ireland, Joyce's lapse may represent less a failure of scholarship and more a desire to claim for his homeland not only defiance of Rome (as Joyce tells us, Scotus "kept a grain of good sense in his exalted brain" and escaped Paris for Ireland), but also a fundamental streak of rebellion that informs its collective heritage. If nothing else, Joyce clearly wishes to argue for the supreme intellectual abilities of "Scotus," and two paragraphs later writes the following: "Two or three illustrious names shine here like the last few stars of a radiant night that wanes as dawn arrives. According to legend, John Duns Scotus, of whom I have spoken before, the founder of the school of Scotists, listened to the arguments of all the Doctors of the University of Paris for three whole days, then rose and, speaking from memory, refuted them one by one" (CW, 161). Because this information comes in its own paragraph Joyce may be discriminating the two Scotuses, although his phrase "of whom I have spoken before" remains ambiguous; he has mentioned both names previously. Joyce's point lies in his attempt to establish Ireland's "ego" as formed from medieval intellectual tradition and receptive to the apophatic theology of Dionysian mysticism.

From an examination of national disposition in light of cultural history and religion Joyce concludes that Ireland draws its intellectual identity from its medieval sensibility. In the course of his argument Joyce abandons any notion of a quintessential Irish race, pointing instead to the conglomeration of races that have always composed Ireland. In so doing, he suggests that nationality and heritage may be predicated on matters utterly transcendent:

Nationality (if it really is not a convenient fiction like so many others to which the scalpels of present-day scientists have given the coup-de-grace) must find its reason for being in something that surpasses and transcends and informs changing things like blood and the human word. The mystic theologian who assumed the pseudonym of Dionysius, the pseudo-Areopagite, says somewhere, "God has disposed the limits of nations according to his angels," and this probably is not a purely mystical concept. Do we not see that in Ireland the Danes, the Firbolgs, the Milesians from Spain, the Norman invaders, and the Anglo-Saxon settlers have united to form a new entity, one might say under the influence of a local deity? And, although the present race in Ireland is backward and inferior, it is worth taking into account the fact that it is the only race of the entire Celtic family that has not been willing to sell its birthright for a mess of pottage. (*CW*, 166)

Issues of nationalism aside, Joyce here employs at least a degree of irony regarding the role of the divine in establishing native borders. But he makes quite clear that human variables such as lineage and language do not determine the construction of a national identity. Joyce's call for a criterion that "surpasses and transcends and informs" human form perhaps finds its answer in his invocation of Dionysius. Despite his skeptical belief that the relationship between angels and nations "probably is not a purely mystical concept," Joyce predicates national identity upon intangibilities that resemble mystical ineffability. In the essay on William Blake mystical practice entails the release of personality and difference, not the erection of mental and physical boundary. In the present parlance, the invaders of Ireland coalesce to form "a new entity . . . under . . . a local deity," thus predisposing the national consciousness to see its origins and temperament as divinely (or, at least, medievally) ordered.

The essay concludes with reflections upon émigrés, the "wild geese" who fled modern Ireland's repressiveness. To sum up his response to the present artistic and rebellious state of Ireland, Joyce invokes Oscar Wilde as the ultimate model of the émigré and central model for his own expatriotism. Stating that "old Ireland" is dead, Joyce argues that one must not look to a past artistic vitality as pardon for the present-day lassitude of the country. Repeating Wilde's praise of Irish loquaciousness, Joyce suggests that, much like nationhood, "revolution is not made of human breath and compromises" and that speedy cultural reform must occur. The final sentence demonstrates Joyce's attitude toward Ireland, Wilde, exile, and national consciousness. Figuring the early modern renaissance of Irish culture as either revival from the dead, or the staging of a theatrical production, Joyce observes: "I am sure that I, at least, will never see that curtain go up, because I will have already gone home on the last train."

This "last train" of exile draws Joyce to the very heart of his rebellion against Church, state, and constricting Irish identity. In his essay entitled "Oscar Wilde: The Poet of Salome," he suggests that the responsibility for Wilde's persecution and subsequent exile to France lay in the morality of the English, who sent up a "howl of puritanical joy" at the exposure of his homosexuality. Joyce declares quite pointedly that Wilde's so-called guilt was, in a social sense, irrelevant. Rather, in the eyes of Edwardian England the point of Wilde's scandal lay in the unseemliness of its exposure. For these reasons Joyce presents Wilde as a scapegoat, the "inescapable product of the Anglo-Saxon college and university system, with its secrecy and restrictions" (*CW*, 204). With a poetic sensibility derived partly from Pater and Ruskin, this Irish "court-jester" to the English public appears, in the course of the essay and in the language of Joyce's analysis, to draw his artistic inspiration from a source similar to that of other Irish writers—spiritual orientation. Describing Wilde's deathbed conversion to Rome, Joyce writes of "the singer of the divinity of joy" who, saddened by death, "closed the book of his spirit's rebellion with an act of spiritual dedication" (*CW*, 203). This passage demonstrates the strain of theology by which Joyce makes sense of Wilde's work, and death. After identifying the English social system as the greatest culprit in Wilde's persecution, the essay turns to Dorian Gray as the embodiment of the "pulse" of his art— "sin." This "pulse" beats with much the same implication as the "systole and diastole of love" by which Joyce identifies the attraction of Dionysius in the essay on William Blake. This attraction is the allure of "beauty," "subjective interpretations of Aristotle," and the "truth inherent in the soul of Catholicism: that man cannot reach the divine heart except through that sense of separation and loss called sin" (*CW*, 205). Understood through the implications and resonances of Joyce's analysis, Wilde's conversion articulates for early modern aesthetics the conceptual separation, loss, absence, and creativity inherent in mystical theology.

James Clarence Mangan, like Wilde, cast aesthetic ideals in theological terms. In "Ireland, Isle of Saints and Sages," Joyce states in a tone of sentimental finality: "The old national soul that spoke during the centuries through the mouths of fabulous seers, wandering minstrels and Jacobite poets disappeared from the world with the death of James Clarence Mangan. With him, the long tradition of the triple order of the old Celtic bards ended; and today other bards, animated by other ideals, have the cry" (*CW*, 173–74). In 1902 Joyce had already written on Mangan, and in 1907 delivered a lecture in partial revision of that earlier work. Joyce here identifies Mangan with the failed promises of Irish literature. In the first of the essays Joyce strove to present the aesthetic requirements of Ireland in terms of the medieval and spiritual influ-

ences present in the author's work. The essay begins with a discussion
of the tensions between classical and romantic art. Joyce focuses upon
the ineffable transcendence that he believes to be of essence to Mangan and to early modernism. The essay describes Mangan's sensitive,
dreamy nature with which "the lore of many lands goes . . . always,
eastern tales and the memory of curiously printed medieval books
which have rapt him out of time" (*CW,* 77). By adopting Paterian style
and motif Joyce portrays Mangan's imagination as evolving from aesthetic tenets that are, by implication, medieval in origin. Although
Mangan lacks the "faith of the solitary, or the faith, which in the middle
age, sent the spires singing up to heaven," he nonetheless epitomizes
the intellectual qualities of literature that emerge from internal, private
explorations of human experience. As Joyce states, "poetry, even when
apparently most fantastic, is always a revolt against artifice, in a sense,
against actuality" (*CW,* 81). In this definition of the nature of poetry,
consonant with the artistic goals of much late Victorian literature, the
primacy of logic, reason, materiality, and temporality gives way, and
the functions of memory and history dissolve. The quote continues: "It
[poetry] speaks of what seems fantastic and unreal to those who have
lost the simple intuitions which are the tests of reality; and, as it is often
found at war with its age, so it makes no account of history, which is
fabled by the daughters of memory, but sets store by every time less
than the pulsion of an artery, the time in which its intuitions start forth,
holding it equal in its period and value to six thousand years. No doubt
they are only men of letters who insist on the succession of the ages,
and history or the denial of reality, for they are two names for one thing,
which may be said to be that which deceives the whole world" (*CW,*
81). The artist must construct a resistance to the rational processes of
memory and history. In the later, 1911 essay on Blake, Joyce employed
precisely the same metaphor of pulsation, the "systole and diastole of
love," to suggest the collapse of time and ordinary referents in the
course of describing the processes of the mind and the mysticism of
Dionysius. Joyce implies that these revelations of the mind to itself, and
of the literature of a people to themselves, find their roots in the ineffable and spiritual. All ages must seek "sanction" in their poetry and
philosophy, "for in these the human mind . . . attains to an eternal state"
(*CW,* 82), and the essay concludes in a rhapsodic celebration of the possibilities of mystical philosophy for these artistic ends. This unity with
eternity becomes the subject of the essay's conclusion, and, echoing the
mystical tradition of John of the Cross, Joyce describes with enthusiasm
the cycles of divinity, darkness, and artistic illumination that beget the

state of mind in which the "imagination contemplates intensely the truth of its own being" and in which all will partake in the "continual affirmation of the spirit" (*CW*, 83).

Joyce's 1907 revisions to the first essay on Mangan emphasized the poet's dissolute life and and artistic limitations. Delivered shortly after "Ireland, Isle of Saints and Sages," this essay ironically notes that to the "detriment" of the "noted generosity of the Emerald Isle," Mangan has not been enshrined as a literary hero. Joyce suggests that the poet does indeed represent the best of nineteenth-century Celtic revivalism. While Joyce describes the alcoholic and opiate-induced behavior that characterized Mangan's writing and life, he retains the earlier invocations of medieval, mystical sensibilities as the hallmark of his aesthetic practice. Satirizing in part his own earlier Paterian phrasing, Joyce nonetheless retains the sense of Mangan's theological orientation emphasized in the first essay. The "spiritual yearnings and imaginary loves of the Middle Ages" control Mangan's imagination, and his poetry exists "under a veil of mysticism." To the praise of Mangan as a poet who "sums up in himself the soul of a country," Joyce adds that "although he was the spiritual focus of his time, he refused to prostitute himself to the rabble or to make himself the loud-speaker of politicians. He was one of those strange abnormal spirits who believe that their artistic life should be nothing more than a true and continual revelation of their spiritual life, who believe that their inner life is so valuable that they have no need of popular support, and thus abstain from proffering confessions of faith, who believe, in sum, that the poet is sufficient in himself, the heir and preserver of a secular patrimony, who therefore has no urgent need to become a shouter, or a preacher, or a perfumer" (*CW*, 184). One suspects that the "perfumer" of the last line ought to be "performer." Nevertheless, the above quote strikingly unites Joyce's preoccupations with the spirit of an era, the character of the Irish nation, and the temperament of the artist. Here, as elsewhere, this heritage is the "patrimony" of cultural and theological history, rebellion against authority, and preoccupation with the interior life of the mind as the nexus of aesthetics. Much like Stephen in *Portrait*, Joyce ordains the artist as the secular "priest of the eternal imagination" (*P*, 221).

In *The Aesthetics of Chaosmos* Umberto Eco acknowledges the importance of the 1907 essay on Mangan for suggesting the contours of Joyce's early thought. He notes that Joyce focused on the decadent, opium-eating aspect of Mangan's personality because he wished to write about the imagination in a state of unbridled excitement. Commenting on the relationship between creativity and aesthetic theory, Eco writes: "While

Joyce provides an exact description of our daily humanity . . . at the same time he discovers in Mangan an example of the revelatory function of poetry. Once again, the artist can succeed in possessing and communicating the truth, but only through beauty. Thus the situation is reversed. When Joyce speaks of beauty as the splendor of truth in the essay on Mangan, he no longer thinks of a truth that—qua truth—becomes beauty, but of a gratuitous beauty, born from the provocative strength of the imagination which, in fact, becomes the only possible truth" (Eco, 13). In this definition of the nature of beauty and the function of poetry Mangan embodies Pater's subjective aesthetic. Although Eco concludes his observations by noting "the symbolist poets and mystics" that enable *Portrait*'s "amazing convergence of three diverse attitudes—realism, decadence, and the scholastic forma mentis" (Eco, 14), he does not elucidate their relationship to Paterian thought or the Victorian appropriation of medieval aesthetics. To Joyce, Pater represents the most encompassing figure for a discussion of the role of mystical theology in the presentation of interior consciousness, the understanding of perception, and the subjective nature of reality. Pater is the most central transitional writer from the late-nineteenth-century world of Mangan, Wilde, and the poets of the continent to the twentieth-century intellectual world of Joyce's fiction.

In the most basic sense, Pater explains the allure of theology to those who "through religion, have become dead to religion" (De Laura, 195). In the absence of traditional religious authority Pater sees "some feature of the ancient religious life" surviving in the "modern artist or philosopher." This guiding intellectual, emotional, and spiritual principle, he says, is the "ideal of a transcendental disinterestedness," or what David De Laura calls "religious aestheticism." Joyce's articulation of exactly this high aesthetic "disinterestedness," like one of Stephen's characterizations of God in *Portrait* as "indifferent, paring his fingernails," has earned undeserved reproof as representative of ideological lassitude. Ruth Child's words on this subject in her critical commentary on Pater apply equally to the later decadent aesthete, Joyce; in effect, she maintains that the task of the critic is less to lament aestheticism's apparent distance from social values than to identify why Pater (and Joyce) concerns himself so much with sensation and perception (Child, 1). For this reason the key to Pater lies in understanding perception as a feature of the revelation of the mind to itself. In *The Renaissance* it expresses itself in the sculpture of Greece, the painting and mysticism of the Middle Ages, and the music and poetry of the modern era (*Renaissance*, 180–84). This perception and revelation constitute the "religious phase possible for the modern mind," which Pater acknowledges to be the "main object of [his] design to convey" (Benson, 90).

That Joyce knew Pater's work, and that his own writing may resemble certain portions of it, should come as no surprise. Both authors read eclectically and similarly. By 1866, Pater had read Vico, and by 1869, according to Billie Andrew Inman, had assimilated Origen, Cyrenaic philosophy, Bruno, and Saint Francis of Assisi. Inman maintains that the influence of Vico may be observed in the cyclicality of "ascesis" and decadence that occupies Pater's writing; in any case, he observes that Pater regularly pointed out the ancient forebears of modern ideas. On the subject of mysticism itself Inman records two responses that especially reveal Pater's confluence of art and theology in a very Joycean way. In a review of William Morris' poems Pater declares that the "apex of mystic religion" is Dante. In another piece he states that for Rousseau, as for Christian mystics, religion merges "into sensuous love, and sensuous love into religion." In both of these observations, Pater identifies mysticism as contributing to the philosophy of memory, imagination, and perception and thus shapes a discussion of sensation and aesthetics according to its dimensions.[3]

In the essay "Style" Pater is most succinct about the role of the philosophy of the mind in writing. Although he concerns himself with the function of scholarship in establishing standards of writing, he attributes the development of pleasing style to the subjective nature of fact and the labor of the acute mind. The true literary artist must try to present things as they "really" are, despite human limitations on knowledge and language's own restrictions. Pater asserts that language possesses its own life and that scholars must acknowledge its development. He notes that "English, for a quarter of a century past, has been assimilating the phraseology of pictorial art; for half a century, the phraseology of the great German metaphysical movement of eighty years ago; in part also the language of mystical theology" (*Style,* 12). Pater himself adopts this language of mystical theology to describe the way in which the alert reader derives pleasure from the most painstaking, highly crafted style: "a skilful economy of means, *ascesis,* that too has a beauty of its own" (*Style,* 14). Citing Flaubert as the writer most inclined to choose *le mot juste,* Pater subtly elaborates the structural metaphor for the mind that he uses throughout the essay to indicate the manner in which "the literary architecture," defined as "a single, almost visual image," upholds the "necessity of mind in style." In this manner Pater indicates that, properly conceived, a literary work generates its own image and its own conclusion; in effect, it is teleological, containing its origins and endings. The individual, apprehending mind that Pater upholds as the model of consciousness has within itself the potential to communicate the larger structure of reality. This concept, in its fashioning of time, history, and the outside world, resonates with the same models of consciousness found in John of the Cross's rendering of the body and mind in prayer. Indeed, Pater comments of Flaubert's structurally complete work that "the house he has built is rather a body he had informed" (*Style*, 21).

While the operations of mind in style lead Pater to a secular religiosity in his description of the artistic process, the presence of soul in style leads him to a religious secularity, in which the soul describes the means by which certain writers absorb language "through vagrant sympathy and a kind of immediate contact." In short, he states that it is the "way in which theological interests sometimes avail themselves of language" that best indicates the nature of soul and "lends to profane writers a kind of religious influence" (*Style*, 23). Although Pater resists a vision of total subjectivity—after all, his is a critique of the greatness of art—he does present literature as the product of a privileged moment of consciousness, a kind of revelation. In "Wordsworth" he declares that the "end of life is not action but contemplation—*being* as distinct from *doing*" and that artists are the masters of the "art of impassioned contemplation" (*Style*, 62). The religious sentiment that governs the imagination "has always had much to do with localities, with the thoughts which attach themselves to actual scenes and places," and this meditation on a specific memory and place is characteristic not only of earlier mystical writers like Ignatius of Loyola in his composition of place, but also of its avowed subject, literary artists like Joyce. The conclusion to "Style" summarizes the criterion for literary greatness as that which ennobles and which contains "mind and soul—that colour and mystic perfume, and that . . . architectural place, in the great structure of human life" (*Style*, 36).

Pater's intellectual system underpins the philosophical construction of modernism. Carolyn Williams observes that "Pater saliently argues that modernism is a recurrent phenomenon in history" (Williams, 2). In this concept, history itself, much like the national history engaged by Joyce, does not exist empirically but must be reconstructed from the individual temperament, disposition, and recollection—"personal memory and historical retrospection" (Williams, 10). This notion of interior understanding leads directly to the "modern" heart of Pater's Victorianism in the form of an investigation of the inescapability of uncertainty. As Williams later says, "by relating every object to its uneasy grounding in an isolated and ephemeral subject, Pater presents scientific objectivity and romantic epistemology as two opposing but correlative modes of deriving the radically relativist position at the extremes of 'modern thought' . . . Pater's simultaneously late Romantic, late Victorian, and early modern position in the English literary tradition may be seen in this intensified awareness that the problems of 'objective' knowledge and the problem of 'subjectivity' are intractably one and the same problem" (Williams, 25). Although Williams and others analyze this problem in terms of his German Romantic heritage, Pater himself figures the tension between subject and object, perception and understanding as emerging from the context of the Middle Ages. So while Pater begins *The Renaissance* with the maxim that the goal of criticism is "to see the object as in itself it really is," the essays comprise an investigation of what it means to know "one's own impression" as it really is. The pose of objectivity gives way, and the nature of reality turns on a crisis of self-awareness that Pater likens to epistemological distinctions among classical, medieval, and Renaissance art.

The introduction to *The Renaissance* supremely presents the subjectivity of pleasure and the resistance to actuality that compose Pater's most basic sense of mystical discernment and the limits of understanding. Pater consistently associates the word *mystic* with a vaguely defined medievalism, and uses these terms to convey his sense of the nature of consciousness. In "Pico della Mirandola" Pater comes closest to a definition of the term: "The word *mystic* has been usually derived from a Greek word which signifies *to shut*, as if one *shut one's lips*, brooding on what cannot be uttered; but the Platonists themselves derive it rather from the act of *shutting the eyes*, that one may see the more, inwardly" (*Renaissance*, 28). This sense of the visual powerfully relates to the formation and dissolution of image at the center of negative prayer and the relationship between sensory denial and spiritual enlightenment offered by the tradition of Dionysius. Pater's configuration of mysticism matches that of Joyce in its ability to communicate, despite its denial of the senses, a deeper affiliation with the creative life of the mind; Pater, like Joyce, perceives religion and sensuous love merging in the Christian mystic, and both perceive in the mystic the prototype of artistic consciousness, able to fabricate image from word and word from image.

To Pater this inward vision enables the pictorial inventiveness of the Italian Renaissance by correlating Provençal art with the "pleasures of the sense and the imagination" (*Renaissance*, 19). Yet, as in the case of Leonardo, the eye of memory and personality "seems . . . to reflect ideas and views and some scheme of the world within; so that he seemed to his contemporaries to be the possessor of some unsanctified and secret wisdom; as to Michelet and others to have anticipated modern ideas" (*Renaissance*, 78). In his evocation of Leonardo's muse, Pater retreats to a description of the momentary and evanescent qualities of imagination as the external world gives way and the eye looks incursively in a manner anticipatory of his Conclusion: "Through Leonardo's strange veil of sight things reach him so; in no ordinary night or day, but as in faint light of eclipse, or in some brief interval of falling rain at daybreak, or through deep water" (*Renaissance*, 87). The painting of Leonardo derives from the "world within," whose interiority allows for the expression of the art of memory and time. Music, the condition to which all poetry will aspire, in its most "delightful" mode "seems to be always approaching to figure, to pictorial definition . . . there being a poetry also of memory and of the mere effect of time" (*Renaissance*, 105). This poetry of memory and time resists literality and actuality, instead equipping the artist, like John of the Cross, to transcend the senses through the senses. In the "Winckelmann" essay this transformation takes the form of the shift from Greek sensual indulgence to "the mystical art of the Christian middle age, which is always struggling to express thoughts beyond itself" (*Renaissance*, 163). This "exaggerated inwardness" forms the essence of modern sensibility. The concrete substance of classical art, exhumed by the Renaissance mind of Winckelmann, has yet to undergo the "defiance of form" characteristic of the Middle Ages; in the words of Pater, "it has not yet plunged into the depths of religious mysticism" (*Renaissance*, 165). Although Romantic culture offers a partial retreat from the solitude of such inward contemplation, the premise of the chapter resolutely suggests that "the development of various forms of art has corresponded to the development of the thoughts of man concerning humanity, to the growing revelation of the mind to itself" (*Renaissance*, 184). This revelation encapsulates the most elemental part of Pater's philosophy; the "inward world of thought and feeling" expressed in the original Conclusion presents a world in which inner sensation is superior to the world of exterior, provisional reality. This inner sensation finally gives way to the radical subjectivity at the unstable core of experience.

The Conclusion contains the most comprehensive and radical statement of Pater's representation of consciousness to emerge from his consideration of the nature of imagination over time and through private experience. The preparatory quote from Heraclitus, "All things give way; nothing remaineth," introduces the uncertainty of the senses as the basis of personality and reality. All stability and fixity dissolve, and the impressions of others and ourselves compose the isolation of consciousness, with "each mind keeping as a solitary prisoner its own dream of a world" (*Renaissance*, 188). While Pater himself withdrew this Conclusion from the second edition of *The Renaissance*, presumably because of its implicit call to hedonism and self-indulgence, its greater radicalism lies in its denial of knowledge and order as typically conceived. To live only for "moment's sake" is, in effect, to live exclusively within (or without) memory and subjectivity. The creative act becomes akin to the moment of infused contemplation, which requires the absence of will, cognition, and sensation. Pater's implied teleology of consciousness suggests that the evolution of sensibility allows to the modern mind discrete, epiphanal moments of intense awareness, and nothing more; John of the Cross's sketch asserts that at the summit of the mount there is nothing, and that nothing is more.

If *The Renaissance* explores art history from the perspective of the development of human consciousness, *Marius the Epicurean* traces the religious formation of Marius' (and Stephen Dedalus') eternal imagination. As Germain d'Hangest observes in his massive study of Pater, the aesthete thought of "les réalités quotidiennes comme les éléments d'une vaste liturgie" (d'Hangest, 292) and understood perception, indeed reality, as located in the temple of the mind. The exposition of *Marius* reveals the logic by which its hero, progenitor of Stephen Dedalus, reconciles mystical Christianity and sensual pleasure. According to David De Laura, Florian's portrait allows for the "admissibility of Christianity into the unity of culture" and provides the basis for the "sensate religion" to serve as the foundation of *Marius*. As he states, "Christian sacramentalism, 'aesthetic worship,' is seen as canceling the distinction between spirit and matter, obviously on analogy with the fusion of matter and form in art" (De Laura, 262). One can see the relevance of Pater's own commentary in *Appreciations* for the relationship of art and religion: "Practically, the church of the Middle Age by its aesthetic worship, its sacramentalism, its real faith in the resurrection of the flesh, had set itself against that Manichean opposition of spirit and matter, and its results in men's way of taking life; and in this, Dante is the central representative spirit" (*Style*, 212). Although De Laura finally sees Pater as unable to overcome the dualism presumably inbuilt in the human psyche, *Marius* expresses pleasure and sensation as the center of spiritual life. For this reason *Marius* is one of the central texts for Joyce's accommodation of theology to the artistic temperament. William Buckler, amid observations about the relationship of history to the construction of the self in Pater's work, observes the following of his inherent modernity: "What Pater did for the twentieth century . . . was to channel a full-bodied intellectual, spiritual, aesthetic inheritance into a temperament, a portrait, of the artist, broadly conceived, 'perfecting' a life in a work of art called *Marius the Epicurean*" (Buckler, *Walter Pater*, 270). Joyce develops his portrait of the artist from the cloistral images of the Middle Ages that fill the mind of Pater.

Marius traces the development of the religious and psychological life of a young boy. Criticism of the novel either defends its coherence and unity, or suggests that its value lies in its ability to bridge Victorian and modern modes of writing. Both of these approaches only begin to address the central position of this text for the works of Pater and for nineteenth century spiritual biography in general. It is useful to think of similarities to Joyce's later *Portrait*. Like Stephen, Marius begins early in life to evaluate the role of religion, family, and culture for himself and for society. Written in a manner more descriptive than narrative, the account of his youth suggests that he was "more given to contemplation than action" and that he was preoccupied with the "realm of the imagination." Like the later Stephen, he constructed a world within, "by the exercise of meditative power" through which a "vein of 'subjective' philosophy" ran (*Marius*, 15). Finally, much like the death of Stephen's mother in *Ulysses*, the death of Marius' mother promotes a kind of meditative introspection upon loss and absence as determiners of reality.

The death of Marius' friend Flavian amplifies the sense of loss and absence that precipitates his crisis of reflection. "Animula Vagula" concentrates most of Marius' philosophical meditations. Stylistically the chapter strongly recalls the Conclusion to *The Renaissance*, in many spots echoing its phrases and concepts about the nature of time and consciousness. Although the death of Flavian promotes an initial crisis of disbelief in the soul and spiritual matters, the language of the chapter, like the book as a whole, repeats the concepts, images, and terms of mystical theology and reveals the tension between the material and the spiritual inherent in Marius' avowed and actual inquiry into metaphysics. The chapter begins with his decision to abandon poetry for a time, instead taking up rigorous philosophic studies, which ward off "the enervating mysticism, then in wait for ardent souls in many a melodramatic revival of old religion or theosophy" (*Marius*, 71). Although Marius claims to reject "religious fantasies" and "mechanical arcana" as masquerade and Platonic philosophy as too abstract, he strives to maintain his "materialist" viewpoint with "the temper of a devotee" (*Marius*, 72). Similarly, his retreat to intellectual meditation is ascetic in its earnestness and severe in its observation, leading him to pay "devout attention" to Heraclitus and his theories of the flux and fluidity of the universe.

After reflection upon this "restless stream" of Heraclitean existence in a manner anticipatory of Pater's student at Oxford, Gerard Manley Hopkins, Marius explores precisely the ideas of consciousness whose discussion originates in the literature of mysticism and continues throughout the work of Hopkins and Joyce. The "negative doctrine" of the perpetual change of objects becomes a "preliminary step towards a large positive system of almost religious philosophy" in which Marius locates reality in the perceiving mind and evanescent moment. He draws not only his concepts but also his rhetoric from the literature of mystical theology in which memory, recollection, and time are human structures that must be forgotten in order to apprehend the divine. Although Marius acknowledges that Heraclitus' system permits a fixity of relationships, he suggests that memory serves as the first step toward the dissolution of all knowledge. The passing of things, "like the race of water in mid-stream," impedes any real fixity until "momentary sensible apprehension of the individual [becomes] the only standard of what is or is not" (*Marius*, 75). Marius' descent into the "despair of knowledge" resists solipsism and becomes, in his view, a positive philosophy largely because his childhood priest playing and adult disposition incline him to consider the first principle and reserve its discussion as "a fine, high, visionary consideration, very remote upon the intellectual ladder, just at the point indeed where that ladder seemed to pass into the clouds" (*Marius*, 76). This metaphor invokes the ladder of knowing so common to the mystical tradition begun by Dionysius and contextualizes his Dedalian view of reality: "And those childish days of reverie, when he played at priests, played in many another day-dream, working his way from the actual present, as far as he might with a delightful sense of escape in replacing the world of other people by an inward world as himself really cared to have it, had made him a kind of 'idealist.' He became aware of the possibility of a large dissidence between an inward and somewhat exclusive world of vivid personal apprehension, and the unimproved, unheightened reality of the life of those about him" (*Marius*, 76). Reverie and daydream resist the actuality of the present and allow the young Marius to develop toward the verbal and visual imagination that later emerges in Stephen Dedalus. To accept the outer world as certain and verifiable through the experiences of others exists "only as a kind of irony"; the most reasonable philosophies of life permit the "primary element of incertitude or negation" as the central condition of humanity.

He accepts his earlier Cyrenaic philosophy as a genial expression of pleasure and respect for existence that nonetheless recognizes the "'subjectivity of knowledge'" and the basis of certainty as a mere "fixity of language" (*Marius*, 79). To Marius, this appreciation of individual consciousness necessitates the "renunciation" of metaphysical speculation and the acceptance of an "anti-metaphysical metaphysic" of "sensuous wisdom" (*Marius*, 81). This act of renunciation ends in an affirmation central to the remainder of the novel and to Pater's larger aesthetic designs: "insight through culture" permits the individual to know "life as the end of life," the maxim toward which the chapter builds. On the beach in *Portrait* Stephen sees language visually and invokes as his artistic ideal the "call" to "recreate life out of life" (*P*, 172). To live this design fully, one must become a "complex medium of reception towards the vision—the 'beatific vision'" of actual experience that changes ordinary reality to accommodate its own private vocation. Marius recognizes the importance of the visual imagination in the training of the mind. As he says, a culture devoted to emotions and sensitivity "might come even to seem a kind of religion—an inward, visionary, mystic piety or religion . . . In this way, the true aesthetic culture would be realizable as a new form of the contemplative life, founding its claim on the intrinsic 'blessedness' of 'vision'" (*Marius*, 85). He continues to desire, "in the mystic *now*," the ability to become an artist—to "arrest for others also, certain classes of experience, as the imaginative memory presented them to himself" (*Marius*, 89). The chapter ends in a tone of pious commitment to study and labor that would produce the priestly "sombre habitude of the avowed scholar" who has been "initiated into a great secret" (*Marius*, 90). *Et ignotas animum dimittit in artes.*

Like his philosophical ancestors Marius associates himself "to the consciousness of God" (*Marius*, 161). Avowedly tied to the concerns of Platonic philosophy, the image of the eternal circle "whose centre is everywhere, the circumference nowhere" (*Marius*, 164) arises as a figure of his conceptualization of God and defines his sense of contemplation as an attempt to ascend the "celestial ladder" of understanding, a metaphor Marius employs to identify the "boldly mystical" view of humanity that he advocates (*Marius*, 193). Almost in anticipation of Stephen's early piety, Marius reflects upon the "aesthetic charm of the catholic church, her evocative power over all that is eloquent and expressive in the better mind of man, her outward comeliness, her dignifying convictions about human nature:—all this, as abundantly realized centuries later by Dante and Giotto, by the great medieval church-builders, by the great ritualists like Saint Gregory, and the masters of sacred music in the middle age—"(*Marius*, 210–11). In this montage of future history Marius anticipates and applauds precisely those features of religious culture that he considers to be the *"necessary"* products of the mind and which, in his view, transform the liturgy to take "exclusive possession of the religious consciousness. (*Marius,* 213). Marius folds the consciousness of God into the artistic imagination and views the aesthetic object as the product of sensory and sacramental knowledge. The final pages of the novel focus on reproduction, sleep, and burial. The annointing of Marius' "passage-ways of the senses" implies that the final act of perception and consciousness, similar to that of the world in *Finnegans Wake,* occurs during the transformation of death: in the final words of *Marius,* it is "a kind of sacrament with plenary grace" (*Marius,* 267).

While Pater's writing applies the tradition of mysticism to twentieth-century aesthetics, the critical response to Francis Thompson's poetry illustrates the nineteenth century's literary reception of mystical literature. Unlike Pater, Thompson does not alter theology to accommodate the subjectivity of consciousness; rather he looks to tradition to explain his more modern sense of understanding. His most enduring poem, "The Hound of Heaven," employs imagery and stylistic devices that borrow from the literature of John of the Cross (an avowed inspiration), the Bible, and other sources. His techniques resonate with the rhetorical devices of the Metaphysicals and at times anticipate the innovations of Gerard Manley Hopkins. The poem begins with an inversion of the conceit of the lover pursuing the beloved, which emblemizes the contemplative sought out by God. In this model the hound, the metaphor for God's pursuit of the soul, chases down the "arches of the years" and "labyrinthine ways" of the speaker's "mind" in defiance of time and space. The speaker attempts to escape the beast, each time finding salvation in his own recognition that God prohibits his elusiveness. The speaker's Hopkins-like realization that the "designer infinite" must "char the wood ere [he] can limn with it," and that he is in a spiritually broken state, his "freshness spent," provides the transitional point of the poem. The speaker recognizes his mortality and listens to the "Voice" that surrounds him and tells him that only divine love, restored after a spell of absence, gives hope, meaning, and ease to human life.

The poem enjoyed great popularity. It was published in 1893; from 1912 to 1928 critical, biographical, and exegetical studies proliferated, the latter by priests interested in demonstrating the usefulness of the text for meditative purposes. Thompson embodied the essence of spirituality so profoundly for the late nineteenth and early twentieth centuries that Evelyn Underhill calls him "the greatest mystical poet of mod-

ern times," familiar to thousands of readers. Thompson, who took an
interest in contemplation and wrote a life of Ignatius of Loyola, built
into his poem stages of spiritual desolation and regeneration that correspond with the week-by-week recommendations in *Spiritual Exercises*. His enthusiasts produced indulgent biographies, like that of John
Thomson, that dwell upon the genuineness of his Catholicism and the
resonances of his language. Thomson published two accounts of the
poet in 1912, *Francis Thompson: The Preston-Born Poet* and *Francis Thompson: Poet and Mystic*. The second title is almost exactly the same book,
but ran to a third printing. The cult of Thompson valued not only his
artistic talents but also his piety, granting him status as a kind of disci-
plined contemplative whose "mental deportment" avoided the confused thinking of contemporary self-styled mystics (Meynell, 198).

   Although Thompson's popular status is that of a divine, one of the
most intriguing critiques of his poetry sets it in the context of Bergson,
psychoanalysis, and the artistic process. R. L. Megroz argues that the
language of sleep and dreams bears a close relationship to that of the
mystics because both are approximations of a state of consciousness devoted to apprehension. Quoting Bergson, he states: " 'Perceiving for the
sake of perceiving' is, in brief, the state of illumination, in which the
artist creates and the mystic, it may be, intermittently, dwells. If to
eliminate and select is to be awake, the artist and the mystic are awake;
they employ the intellect to transcend the limitations of the practical
reason." In this manner the "mystics are the scientists of disinterested
experience; they are the supreme artists of the will" (Megroz, 172). The
quote by Bergson recalls the state of abstraction in which Marius lives
and that Pater equates to reality and perception. The artist as disinterested mystic again suggests Stephen in *Portrait* and the role of the artistic divine in the creative evolution of the world.

   The writings of another late Victorian, James Thomson, equally absorb themselves in the nature of the soul, God's beneficence, and the
possibilities of human redemption, but with enormous differences in
technique and conclusions. James Thomson achieved notoriety for his
prose writings, which darkly satirized Victorian society and aimed to
dissolve the ascendancy of "Bumbleism"—the "dullness, dishonesty,
conservatism and complacency" of the nineteenth century (Schaefer,
James Thomson, 5). His long poem "The City of Dreadful Night" explores spiritual abandonment, emptiness, and desolation, a version of
the dark night of the soul that sees the mind and its artistic processes as
forsaken. The motif of ever-changing topography of the city at night
and the shifting status of vision and intuition on the part of the speaker

point to the futility of human endeavor and belief. His poetry explores the psychology of pessimism and suggests that the encounter with the nothingness of the urban landscape corresponds to the conceptual void of consciousness at the center of the negative mystical experience. Thomson's poem delineates the process of perception against the futility of human action. He discusses the mind in terms of images and concepts originating in the literature of the mystics but implies, contrary to his mystical borrowing, that life is relentlessly unregenerate. He inherits the tradition, original to the Bible, of the literature of pessimism, but eschews the kind of solace found in its implicit promise of faith. His poem represents the clearest adaptation of mysticism by a nihilistic mind that nonetheless finds it relevant to the experience of consciousness.

The poem begins in the desert with the speaker in a posture of contrition. He articulates the equivalent of the spiritual dark night of absence and despair by evoking a variety of desolate landscapes and interiors. The setting equates the city at night with the speaker's consciousness: "For life is but a dream whose shapes return . . . In their recurrence with recurrent changes / A certain seeming order; where this ranges / We count things real; such is memory's might" (I.3.14–21). Experience, cognition, and reality itself inhere in the folds of the mind; recollection is subject only to its own ceaseless processes and the certitude of death. He evokes a shifting tableau in which the normal senses divest themselves of power and instead permit a kind of discernment through intuition, very similar to the kind of night of sensory deprivation encouraged by John of the Cross: "And soon the eye a strange new vision learns; . . . Yet clearly in this darkness it discerns . . . The ear, too, with silence vast and deep / Becomes familiar though unreconciled; / Hears breathings as of hidden life asleep, / And muffled throbs as of pent passions wild" (III.2–3). This buried life reveals that the numbing of the senses, the "Death-in-Life" of the following stanza, accurately describes his state of consciousness while at the same time hearkening to the tradition of detachment in mystical literature.

In the next section the poem's cinematic eye rests upon the prophet who has come to the desert of consciousness. The incantatory quality of his speech assumes the tone of biblical witness, with the repeated refrain "As I came to the desert it was thus" initiating each section of consuming fire and savage environment, the sun a "bleeding, eyeless socket" and the "enormous things" swooping past "with savage cries and clanking wings." The section resembles the hallucinatory episodes of surrealism and recalls *La Tentation de Saint Antoine* of Flaubert. The hellfire relents with the appearance of a shrouded woman with whom the speaker eventually vanishes. A similar vision of a shrouded woman whose wake occurs in "the chambers of the mansion of [the speaker's] heart" arises later in the poem. This vision suggests that the literary architecture houses the realm of the imagination as the only alternative to the desolation of reality, the hallucinatory visual capacity the only medium of its expression. In phrasing absolutely reminiscent of Pater, the speaker wonders if "Our isolated units could be brought / To act together for some common end?" only to observe "For one by one, each silent with his thought, / I marked a long loose line approach and wend / Athwart the great cathedral's cloistered square, / And slowly vanish from the moonlight air" (XII.1). In this solitary dream of a world the possibility of unity dissipates as smoothly as the cinematic eye of the speaker moves from the solid cathedral to the moonlit air.

The disintegration of vision prompts another series of meditations in which the phantasms of the imagination and illusion of opium dissolve and expose "this real night." In this stanza sequence the speaker employs a popularized idea of the contemplative to contrast with the shock of naked reality: "From prayer and fasting in a lonely cell, / Which brought an ecstasy ineffable / Of love and adoration and delight: / I wake from daydreams to this real night" (XII.6). The monastic analogy quickly vanishes and the litany of disillusionment continues, shifting in location from church, to brothel, to Eden, to literary endeavor, to political revolution. All human effort results in an extreme awareness of its own futility, permitting only lonely roving by night through an urban wasteland of memories and experiences. Composed between 1870 and 1874, the poem anticipates the writing of the century's close and the nihilism of some modernist thought. The poem's end reiterates the point: "That none can pierce the vast black veil uncertain / Because there is no light beyond the curtain; / That all is vanity and nothingness" (XXI.10). In "The City of Dreadful Night" Thomson uses the concept of desolation and abandonment as the means of increasing the soul's capacity to grasp God but implies that the episodic and grotesque images of the mind yield only alienation; he rejects faith in its own terms. Eliot's unreal city will build its foundation on the "confirmation of the old despair" of the poem's final line; the *nada* of John of the Cross comes to express the void of modern consciousness.

While Thomson conceptualizes nihilism in terms of visual perception, Gerard Manley Hopkins illustrates the manner by which the everyday world transforms into a version of the sacred through the agency of the observer. As both priest and poet, Hopkins articulates a symbiotic relationship between the natural world of sense and creation, holy in itself, and the human function of observation that mimics God's grace by perceiving the intrinsic sacredness of all things. Hopkins attributes to the artist the status of co-creator with God because of the perception of inscape. The physical world exists independently of the perceiving mind; however, the act of perception itself allows understanding beyond the actual surface of the object to reveal its individuality and hence its sacredness. For Hopkins this privileged moment of consciousness exists within and because of theology, especially that of the incarnation, indicating the basis of his aesthetic in a conscious reliance upon the ontological assumptions of mystical literature. Hopkins' euphony and precise description distinguish him as most attuned to the sensory and sensual features of an object, which furnish the acute mind, in a transubstantive moment, with a vision of its transcendence. Although the Dionysian tradition abandons the senses to approach union with God, the featureless divinity nonetheless is made manifest in the incarnation. This central paradox of Christian spirituality informs Hopkins' poetry, which perceives the sensory world to make apparent its holiness through its physical, sensual features. In effect, Hopkins explores the nature of perception and cognition within the terms of his faith and its implications for the philosophy of the mind. Carol Christ notes that in shifting from Pater to Hopkins one moves from the inescapability of subjectivity to the necessity for its transcendence. She states that shift in terms of Hopkins' preoccupation with "particulars experienced sensually," in which the act "of sensuous, particular apprehension is the origin of all of our knowledge and our closest contact with the being of creation and of God" (Christ, 143). Because of Hopkins' absolute foundation in the world of particulars, his kind of vision differs from that of the metaphysical poetry he inherits; rather than realigning intellectual relationships, Carol Christ says, Hopkins enables you to "see differently" (Christ, 136).

"The Windhover" expresses the primacy of sight as a means of indulging in the beauty of creation, which, properly understood, holds within itself the mystery of its own existence. The poem serves as an inquiry into the nature of perception and the process of enlightenment from the point of view of the contemplative mind. The sonnet, dedicated to Christ, describes the flight of the kestrel hawk in its octave, and reserves for the sestet the speaker's reflection upon his observations. The sestet itself divides into two tercets: the first directly makes sense of the bird's flight and its correlative in the natural, human, and spiritual world; the second explains the revelations of the first tercet as part of the rightful order of things in the anagogical mind of the speaker.

Acknowledging this literal level of meaning is critical to understanding the poem's glorification of the act of perception that constructs the concrete, sensual basis of the epiphany. The speaker narrates the octave in the past tense, creating, in the life of the mind, the metaphorical contexts of medieval France, falconry, and skating that characterize the swoop and soar of the flight. Pater tutored Hopkins well; the act of recollection itself constitutes reality for the speaker as he relives the experience of the morning. This structure of knowing reinforces larger forms of spiritual understanding; the contemplative vocabulary of lines 7–8, "My heart in hiding / Stirred for a bird," makes philosophic sense of an otherwise unintentionally humorous line and suggests that the meaning of the bird's flight exists within the consciousness of the observer. The "hiding" of the heart recalls the hiding of the spirit from God in the ladder of knowing, expressed in *The Dark Night of the Soul* as well as in "The Hound of Heaven." Similarly, its "stirring" derives from a long tradition of the impulse of the practiced contemplative toward God. The experience of watching the bird and the fact of its recollection produce an intense yearning toward the divine, suggesting that the consciousness of this observer inclines toward the mystical in its understanding of the world. The first tercet indulges in the glory of the observation of the flight, implying that the sight is thrilling not only because of the analogy between the flight and the resurrection but also because the bird is an actual creature possessing its own integrity. The speaker focuses on the inseparability of these two ways of understanding. The second tercet begins with the declamation "No wonder of it," implying that the previous meditation has rendered clear the mystery of his recollection, the actual flight of the bird and the theological subject of the poem. Shifting his focus to the earth and hearth, the tense to the present, and the form of address to the familiar, the speaker presents the epiphany of regeneration and resurrection as a product not only of the meditative consciousness but also of the act of perceiving the intrinsic nature of things.

Hopkins' poetry concerns itself not only with the means by which the physical world yields up the divine, but also with the degree to which the individuality and inscape of one's own being and disposition contain the pattern of revelation consonant with contemplative experience. In "As Kingfishers Catch Fire" the speaker dwells on the means by which each creature "selves," and "Acts in God's eye what in God's eye he is— / In God's eye acts what in God's eye he is— / Christ." Selving for Hopkins replaces Pater's subjectivity and allows for the investigation of one's own meditation as the most permissible of poetic subjects.

Maria Lichtmann observes that in this absorption in actuality one finds the key to Hopkins' poetry, the "mysticism of ordinary experience" (Lichtmann, 134). This mysticism emerges directly from the literature of spirituality in which "contemplation refers to that paradoxical 'activity' where suddenly, but only after patient, reposeful attention, the object is 'seen' for the first time. The contemplative comes before the object without the mental process of expecting, remembering, and especially desiring. In place of desire and will, there is love and willingness" (Lichtmann, 132). This model of thought forms the basis for the epiphany realized in many of the poems; however, the "love and willingness" describes only one outcome of the meditation that Hopkins explores. The so-called dark sonnets, exemplified by "Carrion Comfort," present a speaker experiencing the desolation of the "dark night of the soul." The speaker figures the crisis of faith as prompting anxiety about the loss of the 'self' amid shifting images of a wrathful God and the possibility of total abandonment. The poem, written retrospectively, grants the speaker surcease through recognition that "That night, / that year Of now done darkness I wretch lay wrestling with (my God!) my God." The individuality of the speaker's mind permits the resolution early in the sonnet that he "can something," only through the course of the poem to reveal the inseparability of his struggle from his own being, which is co-existent with the object of his meditation, God.

Hopkins expresses the relationship between God and humans as at once earthly and regenerate. "That Nature Is a Heraclitean Fire and of the Comfort of the Resurrection" exemplifies this positive sense in which the death of nature's "bonniest . . . clearest-selved spark / Man" finds restitution in the resurrection, a bodily reincarnation into flesh and being. Employing the philosophy of Heraclitus, Hopkins transforms a day after a storm into an emblem of the cycle of water, earth, and air to contrast the resiliency of nature against the mortality of humans. As comfort for this observation, he suggests that the most enduring relationship is that which has its end implicit in its beginning, the perception of which alone constitutes its reality—the incarnation and the resurrection: "In a flash, at a trumpet crash, / I am all at once what Christ is, since he was what I am, and / This Jack, joke, poor potsherd, patch, matchwood, immortal diamond, / Is immortal diamond." The unity of spirit and flesh that makes possible a transformative vision of the world absolutely governs the aesthetic choices of Hopkins, in whose intellectual heritage the epiphanic moments of Joyce lie poised.

Joyce's sense of poetry as written "against artifice . . . against actuality" emerges from a careful balancing of the instabilities of absence, knowledge, and apprehension in the teleological literary structure of the tradition from Pater to Hopkins. Against the uncertainties of perception the late Victorians gave Joyce a vocabulary of self-expression, of the "revelation of the mind to itself," which was extraordinarily sensitive to the visual and verbal subjectivity of pleasure and art. The Victorian way of writing, thinking, and seeing the mind enabled Joyce to develop his ideas of the relation between the inquiry of consciousness and the world of the senses, and to find in the interrelation of mysticism and sensuality the immortal diamond of artistic production.

3

The Esthetic Image

The *Portrait* of Sensation

In *A Portrait of the Artist as a Young Man* Joyce uses the language and concepts of mystical literature to describe the mental, physical, and spiritual revelation of the artistic mind to itself. Joyce demonstrates Stephen's coming to knowledge both naturalistically and subjectively, describing a continuous reality of body and mind suggestive of mystical literature's ordering of consciousness. This orientation links ideas of memory, will, and understanding central to the negative mystical tradition to the sensual imagination's verbal and visual capacity to represent the world in art.

As part of this artistic self-disclosure Joyce adopts the tradition of the spiritual autobiography to relate Stephen's interweaving of sensory experience, ideas, and images. This "fall" into knowledge and humanity is the first step toward creativity in the Romantic paradigm of the artist. In a letter to Harriet Shaw Weaver Joyce anticipates the use he will make of the positive value of knowledge in his later literature: "O felix culpa! St. Augustine's famous phrase in praise of Adam's sin" (Ellmann, *Selected Letters*, 321). As one of the original Christian philosophers of the mind, Augustine speculates, among other things, upon the nature of consciousness and the function of memory in the mind's ability to know God or anything else in the world.[1] The "phoenix culprit" in *Finnegans Wake*'s celebration of artistry begins its metamorphosis with Stephen's recognition that his growing awareness of his own mental processes is the most valuable part of his artistic novitiate. In section 10 of his *Confessions* Augustine considers God omnipresent, yet knowable only through the human capacity for thought, perception, and recollection. All understanding falls into the category of self-knowledge; the desire to encounter divine revelation is therefore at once infinite in its

potential, and humanly finite. The key to understanding this Augustinian idea lies in his discussion of the manufacture of images and his
concept of memory:

Memory preserves in distinct particulars and general categories all the perceptions which have penetrated, each by its own route of entry . . . But who can say
how images are created, even though it may be clear by which senses they are
grasped and stored within. For even when I am in darkness and silence, in my
memory I can produce colours at will . . . These actions are inward, in the vast
hall of my memory . . . There also I meet myself and recall what I am, what I
have done . . . This power is that of my mind and is a natural endowment, but I
myself cannot grasp the totality of what I am. Is the mind, then, too restricted
to compass itself, so that we have to ask what is that element of itself which it
fails to grasp? Surely that cannot be external to itself; it must be within the
mind. How then can it fail to grasp it? This question moves me to great aston-
ishment . . . Nor are the actual objects present to me, but only their images. And
I know by which bodily sense a thing became imprinted on my mind . . . They
are pushed into the background in some interior place—which is not a place.
(Augustine, 186–88).

The saint's words inform Aquinas' later belief that "the mind knows
nothing without a phantasm" (Bundy, 219) and thereby recognizes the
world only through the senses. Yet Augustine does not restrict the mind
to knowledge of what it has perceived but rather suggests that the possibilities of understanding are limitless, informed by the senses but not
bound by actual experience. This model of consciousness places subjectivity at the center of mental experience and marvels at the mind's
ability to transcend the contradictions of interiority and communication in its fusion of sensory apprehension and mental images. Much like
the aesthetic concerns of Dionysius the Areopagite, to whom God and
intellect are out of time and space, the "interior place—which is not a
place" holds within it the possibilities for a kind of image making
whose processes of recollection themselves constitute an act of rendering akin to the making of art.

   This aesthetic orientation derives from Augustine's construction of
God as knowable in the human dimension of sense and sensuality. In
his account of the five spiritual senses, Augustine acknowledges "a
light which space cannot contain . . . sound that time cannot seize . . .
perfume which no breeze disperses . . . food no amount of eating can
lessen, and . . . union that no satiety can part" (Augustine, 183). Infinitude is best described in terms of boundless space and time and human
erotic pleasure. His question "But where in my consciousness, Lord, do
you dwell?" is the Augustinian equivalent of "Where was Moses when

the candle went out?" (*U*, 600). For Joyce, the answer is "in the dark." For Augustine it is in the "very seat" of his mind, where he finds nothing. He concludes that the "Lord God of the mind" exists within yet dwells supreme, immutable, omnipresent, not aloof but intimate with all of the human details of consciousness that are discerned through the body's perceptions. Joyce employs these ideas of visuality to explore literal revelation and figural representation as the central model of the imagination. This application of mystical theology to the mystery of art allows Joyce to present more than the self-revelation of the artist or the objective qualities of reality; rather he employs a philosophical model that suggests that the perceiving mind ideally accommodates both the physical and the mental, the rational and the nondiscursive, at the same time.

Joyce's interest in the process of insight and revelation inspired much critical work on the subject of the epiphany as a theological concept adapted to literary use.[2] A careful definition of the term "epiphany" establishes its relationship to the context of mystical literature and expands its meaning to accommodate the dissolution of subject and object in Stephen's creative process. In its historical sense, the term "epiphany" originated in the Eastern Church and entered Western parlance in 361. As a feast it was originally more important than Christmas, and signified a "visible manifestation of a divine being otherwise invisible." In the West, the term represents the adoration of the Magi; in the East it signifies the baptism of Christ. In the Middle Ages the feast was celebrated with the blessing of baptismal waters and the use of chalk to inscribe the names of the Magi over the doors of homes (*NCE*, 480). Joyce lived in powerful devotion to the aesthetic of revealing hidden reality—sacred or otherwise—and the epiphany exactly correlates the form of the feast to the temper of the artist.

Joyce's own use of epiphany, and his use of the term "epicleti," suggest that he was aware of its historical development.[3] In *Stephen Hero*, Joyce defines the terms to mean a "sudden spiritual manifestation"; however, in its Hopkinsian aspect of "whatness" the term recalls the poet's "instress" of minute detail as the means to describe the infused presence of God in the ordinary, natural world (*SH*, 211). In the same manner Stephen's awareness of the sensory, sensual detail of the world mimics Hopkins' sense of "inscape," by which one perceives the world and comes to spiritual and aesthetic insight. To Joyce, who indeed satirized his own youthful enthusiasm for the term by remarking in *Ulysses* on the "epiphanies written on green oval leaves deeply deep" (*U*, 34) of the younger Stephen, meditation on the world of the everyday held

paramount importance as the subject of fiction. Stephen's wryness indicates that he develops his art from the inspiration of the immediate
world. The distinction of epiphany from epicleti, Joyce's term for the
stories in *Dubliners*, is highly significant for establishing the aesthetic
implied in the feast most central to the development of mystical thought.
Epicleti, the preferred term in the Eastern Church, is the act that effects
transubstantiation.[4] In this scheme, Joyce the writer is godlike; his stories amount to a kind of communion. The theological origins of the
terms suggest that *epicleti* offers a model of the creative process, which
presents an interpenetrated vision of reality harmonious with negative
mystical discourse, in which ordinary distinctions of subject and object
no longer exist.

Portrait's first chapter presents the origins of sensation in Stephen's
fusion of the external and internal world. In this primer of the senses,
reality originates in memory, takes shape in the senses, and informs the
present. The novel opens with his preparation to enter the world of
dark, night, and sleep by listening to a bedtime story, and in the drowse
of consciousness he constructs his world by smell: "When you wet the
bed first it gets warm then it gets cold. His mother put on the oilsheet.
That had a queer smell. His mother had a nicer smell than his father"
(*P*, 7). Stephen recognizes his family through their characteristic actions
and gestures and begins to order the world by association and his growing awareness that ideas and images emerge from fused recollection and
sense. At Clongowes he moves from considering the cold, slimy water
of the ditch to the cozy home where "Mother was sitting at the fire with
Dante waiting for Brigid to bring in the tea. She had her feet on the
fender and her jewelly slippers were so hot and they had such a lovely
warm smell!" (*P*, 10). The mental image shifts from the ditch to home
with no less intensity, suggesting varying degrees of reality the most
authentic of which exists anterior to the immediate moment.

Stephen continues to infuse his experience of Clongowes with images
of home, interweaving earlier ideas and phrases to reinforce the inter-
connections between the present and the past and begin to dissolve
their boundaries. During a math competition Stephen considers the
class teams' colors, which lead him to a reverie in which "a wild rose
might be like those colours and he remembered the song about the wild
rose blossoms on the little green place. But you could not have a green
rose. But perhaps somewhere in the world you could" (*P*, 12). Stephen
consciously remembers the song of the rose, and uses it to imagine possibilities beyond the world of Clongowes, or his childhood, or conventional thought. These reminiscences press language to overcome the

awkwardness of space and time, whose relevancy vanishes with his accretion of experience. During a bout of homesickness he figures his desire to go home against the tension of literal and descriptive language: "But he was not sick there. He thought that he was sick in his heart if you could be sick in that place . . . He leaned his elbows on the table and shut and opened the flaps of his ears. Then he heard the noise of the refectory every time he opened the flaps of his ears. It made a roar like a train at night. And when he closed the flaps the roar was shut off like a train going into a tunnel. That night at Dalkey the train had roared like that and then, when it went into the tunnel, the roar stopped . . . It was nice to hear it roar and stop and then roar out of the tunnel again and then stop" (*P,* 13). Stephen is conscious of the potential for language to represent a metaphorical convergence of mind and body; he recalls the noise of the train and hears in its sound his alienation. His thoughts conform to associational, nonsequential experience.

The loneliness epitomized by the noise in the tunnel finds its intellectual counterpart in Stephen's visualization of the universe against which he figures the incertitude of his being relative to transcendence. Counting the days until his Christmas vacation he considers that the time to go home will arrive because the earth always moves round. This thought allows him to speculate on the nature of the earth, which he envisions as "a big ball in the middle of clouds" (*P,* 15). In this observation, Stephen's quest for understanding reaches beyond the confines of home and family. Fleming's rendition of the earth and clouds as green and maroon recalls Dante's brushes, and suggests that much like Ireland itself, Stephen's psychology must be established amidst the philosophic incertitude of history and remembrance. He situates himself according to the hierarchy of space: "Stephen Dedalus / Class of Elements / Clongowes Wood College / Sallins / County Kildare / Ireland / Europe / The World/ The Universe" (*P,* 15). In writing this great chain of being Stephen omits mention of God: "What was after the universe? Nothing. But was there anything round the universe to show where it stopped before the nothing place began? . . . It would be very big to think about everything and everywhere. Only God could do that" (*P,* 16). In the pattern of negative mystical awareness Stephen imagines himself against vast clouds of unknowing in his first insight into the uncertainties of divine or human things.

Word likewise fails to supplant the intangibilities of image in Stephen's visualization of language: "*Dieu* was the French for God and that was God's name too; and when anyone prayed to God and said *Dieu* then God knew at once that it was a French person that was praying . . .

God understood what all the people who prayed said in their different languages still God remained always the same God and God's real name was God" (*P,* 16). The philosophical and religious discernment that determines Stephen's aesthetic borrows its uncertainties of language from the epistemological structure of the negative mystical tradition. He constructs a world from the void of obscurity and places true faith only in the limits of his knowledge of God, or anything else: "it pained him that he did not know well what politics meant and that he did not know where the universe ended" (*P,* 17). At best he relies upon enmeshed images and sensations drawn from his memory and immediate environment:

There was a cold night smell in the chapel. But it was a holy smell. It was not like the smell of the old peasants who knelt at the back of the chapel at Sunday mass. That was a smell of air and rain and turf and corduroy. But they were very holy peasants. They breathed behind him on his neck and sighed as they prayed. They lived in Clane, a fellow said: there were little cottages there and he had seen a woman standing at the halfdoor of a cottage with a child in her arms, as the cars had come past from Sallins. It would be lovely to sleep for one night in that cottage before the fire of a smoking turf, in the dark lit by the fire, in the warm dark, breathing the smell of the peasants, air and rain and turf and corduroy. But, O, the road there between the trees was dark! You would be lost in the dark. It made him afraid to think of how it was. (*P,* 18)

In this description of the chapel Stephen fuses odor and sensation in his childlike fear of the dark, resonant with the psychological alienation and sense of existential anxiety inherent in the universe's infinity and God's finitude in language. Stephen dwells on the darkness and the possibility of ghosts, determining that "all the dark was cold and strange" in its ghoulish potential (*P,* 19). The portrayal of darkness as a quality of perception that may have odor, heat, and cold furnishes an extraordinary psychological reality suggestive of its imaginative and cognitive role in the process of artistic discernment.

As he matures Stephen's mind constructs language according to the idiosyncrasies of the body to express the uncertainties of adolescent sexual awareness. He speculates upon the literal words "Tower of Ivory, House of Gold,"only to adapt the devotion to Eileen's "long white hands . . . long, and white and thin and cold and soft. That was ivory" (*P,* 36). Later, after the theft of sacristy wine, Stephen reacts with "a faint sickness of awe" at the gall of violating a "strange and holy place"; however, he must also accommodate Athy's statement that the boys may have been punished for "smugging"—schooboy slang for homosexual petting. Although at first it seems that Stephen fails to grasp the term ("what did it mean about the smugging in the square? Why did the five fellows in the higher line run away for that?"), a sense of illicit sex informs the conversation, and he finds himself speculating on the nature of the other boys' transgression—whether it was sexual or religious—by reawakening his idealized sense of Eileen in the language of devotion: "Eileen had long thin cool white hands too because she was a girl. They were like ivory; only soft. One day he had stood beside her looking into the hotel grounds . . . She had put her hand into his pocket where his hand was and he had felt how cool and thin and soft her hand was. She had said that pockets were funny things to have: and then all of a sudden she had broken away and had run laughing down the sloping curve of the path. Her fair hair had streamed out behind her like gold in the sun. *Tower of Ivory. House of Gold.* By thinking of things you could understand them" (*P,* 42–43). Stephen joins the hands of religious rhetoric and sexual inquiry to explain the mysteries of behavior, yet still wonders to himself: "but why the square? You went there when you wanted to do something." While yet in the dark about pockets and smugging, remarkably Stephen couches his questions against the very parameters of knowing, whether of God or Eileen.

He pursues the tension between an actual world of relativity and uncertainty, and the imagination which seeks to present reality to itself. To this end Stephen imbues words and images with the potential to free him from doubt: "Words which he did not understand he said over and over to himself till he had learned them by heart: and through them he had glimpses of the real world about him. The hour when he too would take part in the life of that world seemed drawing near and in secret he began to make ready for the great part which he felt awaited him the nature of which he only dimly apprehended" (*P,* 62). With vocabulary derived from mystical literature and filtered through the medievalism typical of *Marius,* he engages in the romanticized introversion of youth by visualizing himself as an initiate preparing in "secret" for the revelation that he "dimly apprehended." After reading *The Count of Monte Cristo* he imagines himself as the hero, "grown older and sadder," proudly refusing the affections of Mercedes. This fantasy contrasts to the ride in the milkcart in which he acknowledges the sharp realities of his family's growing indigence and his bleak future. Stephen begins to sort out past memories and present possibilities, both of which necessitate retreat into the mind: "the ambition which he felt astir at times in the darkness of his soul sought no outlet. A dusk like that of the outer world obscured his mind as he heard the mare's hoofs clattering along the tramtrack on the Rock Road and the great can swaying and rattling behind him" (*P,* 64). Against the actual dust from the horses he portrays his imaginative "stirring" as part of his greater search "in the real world [for] the unsubstantial image which his soul so constantly beheld. He did not know where to seek it or how: but a premonition which led him on told him that this image would, without any overt act of his, encounter him" (*P,* 65). In his immature fantasy of realized desire he misreads the tradition of passive encounter characteristic of the devotional practices of the negative mystical tradition. In his ascetic ambitions he speculates that he and his beloved would "tryst" in a "secret place . . . surrounded by darkness and silence" (*P,* 65). His fantasy employs the motifs of erotic search, chase, and union, thus powerfully converging spirituality and sexuality in the language of mystical literature.

Stephen's convergence of religious image and sexual reality articulates the sense of void and absence that inaugurates his artistic and spiritual novitiate. In his affection for Emma Clery he creates a monastic persona; on the tram ride home, he thinks of the shawl that covers her as a "cowl" and resists her flirtation. When cast in the school play as a student at Belvedere, he adopts a sober demeanor and takes refuge in his high-mindedness at the teasing of his friends who discover Emma's interest in Stephen: "For him there was nothing amusing in a girl's interest and regard. All day long he had thought of nothing but their leavetaking on the steps of the tram at Harold's Cross, the stream of moody emotions it had made to course through him, and the poem he had written about it" (*P,* 77). Stephen begins to forge art from memory and blend it with present experience. While thinking of his presumably heretical essay about the approach of the soul to its creator, he provides retrospective support for reading his desire to "meet in the real world the unsubstantial image which his soul so constantly beheld" (*P,* 65) in explicitly theological terms. Stephen in "his habits of quiet obedience" subsumes recollection to devotion, in this instance to Emma. Recalling her presence in the audience he takes the stage with pleasure, acting in order to overcome "the innumerable faces of the void" (*P,* 85) in the dark impasse beyond the stagelights that separates the actor from the audience, Stephen from other people. At the play's conclusion Stephen chases Emma, only to find that she is gone. He looks at the ground to calm himself, reflecting on the "horse piss and rotted straw" that is a "good odor to breathe" (*P,* 86). His sense of alienation is soothed by the sensory and concrete, much like the actuality of the milkcart.

Stephen increasingly focuses upon concrete reality as it penetrates the "eyes of his mind" in his accommodation of the sensory, sensual world to the absence at the heart of experience. When he sees the word *foetus* carved onto a desk he is startled because its frankness attests to "a trace of what he had deemed till then a brutish and individual malady of his own mind. His recent monstrous reveries came thronging into his memory. They too had sprung up before him, suddenly and furiously, out of mere words" (*P*, 90). Against this background of sexual guilt, Stephen experiences the first revelatory experience in which his attention focuses on the interplay of light as a visual metaphor: "The sunlight breaking suddenly on his sight turned the sky and clouds into a fantastic world of sombre masses with lakelike spaces of dark rosy light. His very brain was sick and powerless. He could scarcely interpret the letters of the signboards of the shops. By his monstrous way of life he seemed to have put himself beyond the limits of reality" (*P*, 92). Stephen figures himself against the limits of consciousness and cognition—he can scarcely read—and the "dark rosy light" of enlightenment visually defines his artistic enterprise. Fighting against artistic alienation and the void of solipsism, Stephen indulges his family in a season of merrymaking with his essay contest winnings. His wealth, however, is short-lived and he returns to his "futile isolation." He reflects that "he had not gone one step nearer the lives he had sought to approach nor bridged the restless shame and rancour that divided him from mother and brother and sister . . . He felt that he was hardly of the one blood with them but stood to them rather in the mystical kinship of fosterage, fosterchild and fosterbrother" (*P*, 98). In his inability to connect with his family he implies that "mystical kinship" binds in spirit but not in flesh. In this extra sense of alienation he focuses upon his sexual fantasies as the most compelling version of reality—mental and physical—to which he can adhere: "He bore cynically with the shameful details of his secret riots in which he exulted to defile with patience whatever image had attracted his eyes. By day and night he moved among distorted images of the outer world. A figure that had seemed to him by day demure and innocent came towards him by night through the winding darkness of sleep, her face transfigured by a lecherous cunning, her eyes bright with brutish joy. Only the morning pained him with its dim memory of dark orgiastic riot, its keen and humiliating sense of transgression" (*P*, 99). Stephen moves "through the winding darkness of sleep" amid nighttime alterations of reality, fabricating within his mind images of seduction that emerge from his imaginative, erotic transfigurations.

His union of body and mind with unsubstantial image and substantial form stands as a model of interpenetrated experience; he begins to dissolve the boundaries of subject and object by surmounting given reality through his own private understanding. As he says in the rhythmic, repetitive prelude to the chapter's conclusion, he felt "some dark presence moving irresistibly upon him from the darkness, a presence subtle and murmurous as a flood filling him wholly with itself. Its murmur besieged his ears like the murmur of some multitude in sleep; its subtle streams penetrated his being. His hands clenched convulsively and his teeth set together as he suffered the agony of its penetration. He stretched out his arms in the street to hold fast the frail swooning form that eluded him and incited him: and the cry that he had strangled in his throat issued from his lips . . . a cry for an iniquitous abandonment" (*P*, 100). Stephen envisions himself crucified by desire and, in a way reminiscent of John of the Cross's sketch of the ascent of the mount as the arrival at darkness and understanding, expresses his longing as the wish for penetration and abandonment; he merges the aesthetic and ascetic in his fusion of religion, sex, and reality. As in his more romanticized daydreams, he practices a devotion to the chaos of the senses. In his first visit to the brothel he sees groups of women gathered "arrayed as if for some rite. He was in another world: he had awaked as from the slumber of centuries" (*P*, 100). His ordination culminates in the bedroom where the prostitute undresses and begins to kiss him. Although he refuses to kiss her, he describes the sense of surrender and merging that dominates his being in an ultimate model of union through sensuality: "He closed his eyes, surrendering himself to her, body and mind, conscious of nothing in the world but the dark pressure of her softly parting lips. They pressed upon his brain as upon his lips as though they were the vehicle of a vague speech; and between them he felt an unknown and timid pressure, darker than the swoon of sin, softer than sound or odour" (*P*, 101). Stephen's preoccupation with the smell of dark and the sound of loneliness culminates in the synesthesia of the last phrase, whose very assonance suggests the melding and absorption of erotic consciousness that begets a "vague speech" whose words Stephen will learn to articulate through art.

Stephen melds his sexual awareness with the spiritual exegesis at the book's center, wishing, much like Augustine, to be made chaste, but not yet.[5] He discovers sexuality as a form of rebellious pride of intellect, in which lies the key to his self-knowledge and developing model of artistry. Although he adopts repentance at the end of the chapter, his religiosity emerges not so much from piety as from aesthetics, in which his predisposition toward mystical as opposed to doctrinal theology may be discerned. At the beginning of the chapter Stephen thinks of his soul as extinguishing stars and falling back on itself, creating a "cold darkness" that "filled chaos" and left him with a "cold indifferent knowledge of himself" (*P*, 103). Despite his private world of sexual indulgence and his ironic disdain for piety, Stephen remains the prefect of the sodality of the Virgin Mary and keeps on his wall an illuminated scroll whose imagery and attributes appeal to his senses: "The glories of Mary held his soul captive: spikenard and myrrh and frankincense, symbolizing the preciousness of God's gifts to her soul" (*P*, 104). He recalls that his devotion to Mary falls from "lips whereon there still lingered foul and shameful words, the savour itself of a lewd kiss." The realm of the senses determines his religious devotion, appealing to his sense of odor and taste and descriptive of the "darkness" of his search for knowledge. As he says, "he found an arid pleasure in following up to the end the rigid lines of the doctrines of the church and penetrating into obscure silences only to hear and feel the more deeply his own condemnation" (*P*, 106). The sober demeanor of his early adolescence conforms itself to a love of ritual (and rigidity) for its own sake and views worship as penetrating the "obscure silences" of divinity and his own consciousness.

The retreat allows the examination of conscience, reflection on the mysteries of faith, and meditation on one's presence in the universe. Stephen's fusion of "sins, the jeweleyed harlots of his imagination" with the image of Emma prompts a recollection of his "guilty" confessional letters that he plants for girls to read. Despite the secularity of his "confession," he envisions Emma as an accessible deity who grants absolution in union blessed not by God, but by Mary. Stephen arranges his world around women, and as the retreat instruction begins, the priest repeats Satan's "non serviam" in Genesis, thus tracing the root of sin from the fundamental reluctance to serve God's will. The sermon dwells lengthily on the torments of hell, although Stephen's fear of damnation focuses in particular on his self-referentiality as the source of alienation from God. In this respect hell exists within his own mental constructions, capable of lewd imaginings as well as idolatry of Emma. Belvedere is Jesuit-run, and the retreat leader suggests that the boys practice Loyola's composition of place in order to "imagine with the senses of the mind, in our imagination, the material character of that awful place and of the physical torments which all who are in hell endure." Loyola's *Spiritual Exercises* primarily guides one in image-oriented meditative prayer rather than in negative contemplation. In this sermon hell is the pain of conscience and the "memory of past pleasure" (*P*, 128). To Stephen, the making of images derives precisely from memory, sensuality, and pleasure. The priest continues to describe the torments of the underworld by noting the correlation of external and internal reality. Just as the more developed mental faculties derive their stimulation from the senses, so too are they more capable of anguish. In this respect, the mind and understanding may fill with "an interior darkness more terrible even than the exterior darkness which reigns in that dreadful prison" (*P*, 130). The finely attuned mind creates its own torment; hell is acute consciousness.

After the sermon Stephen examines his conscience: "He could not weep . . . He felt only an ache of soul and body, his whole being, memory, will, understanding, flesh, benumbed and weary" (*P*, 136). Stephen locates his consciousness within Bonaventure's categories of mystical intellection—memory, will, and understanding—and parallels his "ache of conscience" with medieval attempts to understand the soul visually: "He desired with all his will not to hear or see. He desired till his frame shook under the strain of his desire and until the senses of his soul closed. They closed for an instant and then opened. He saw" (*P*, 137). The struggle induces a vision of a wasteland lumped with excrement, foul smelling, populated by goatlike creatures who walk slowly through the dung. As he considers the nature of confession, he ponders the origin of sin as the product of visual and bodily responses: "It could happen in an instant . . . By seeing or by thinking of seeing. The eye sees the thing, without having wished first to see. Then in an instant it happens. But does that part of the body understand or what?" (*P*, 139). Stephen centers knowing in the act of perception, here resonant with the sexual guilt under which Stephen labors. The "part of the body" to which he refers is clearly the eye, but with strongly phallic associations: "The serpent, the most subtle beast of the field. It must understand when it desires in one instant and then prolongs its own desire instant after instant, sinfully. It feels and understands and desires . . . Who made it to be like that, a bestial part of the body able to understand bestially and desire bestially?" (*P*, 139–40). Stephen's reaction rewrites Blake's question: Did he who made the imagination make desire? The answer, in mystical literature and Joycean word, is yes; however, Stephen has not yet forged the relationship of this concept to art and instead wishes for union with God as a means of staving off the "black cold void waste" of spiritual abandonment. He confesses, and the chapter ends with the ministration of communion at the end of the retreat.

But Stephen's piety is short-lived. Following the retreat he outwardly conforms to religion but rejects faith in favor of a secularized devotion to art. The "habits of quiet obedience" he cultivated in school transform into an almost obsessive attention to the details and deprivations of the pseudomonastic life he constructs. He envisions himself as an early Christian praying in the catacombs, or as a contemplative whose devotions climb to heaven as "a frail column of incense or as a slender flower." Amid his regime of abstinence and rosary praying he wonders at the nature of true union and enlightenment, and "it seemed strange to him at times that wisdom and understanding and knowledge were so distinct in their nature that each should be prayed for apart from the others" (P, 148). In a similar manner his meditation on the property of the trinity leads him to another fissure in his religious orientation: "The imagery through which the nature and kinship of the Three Persons of the Trinity were darkly shadowed forth in the books of devotion which he read—the Father contemplating from all eternity as in a mirror His Divine Perfections and thereby begetting eternally the Eternal Son and the Holy Spirit proceeding out of Father and Son from all eternity— were easier of acceptance by his mind by the reason of their august incomprehensibility than was the simple fact that God had loved his soul from all eternity" (P, 149). Stephen gravitates toward the incomprehensible texts as more representative of God because he finds the traditional teaching of the Church simplistic and unable to account for the eruptions of his human nature. He concludes that this is the most emotion his soul will experience and that he must, in keeping with his resurgence of faith, "no longer disbelieve in the reality of love" (P, 149). In effect, he practices to the letter a faith that demonstrably does not conform to his perceptions, yet which absolutely determines the function of his mind.

The idea of love informs his decision to abandon faith and take up self-expression through art. He considers "the attitude of rapture in sacred art, the raised and parted hands, the parted lips and eyes as of one about to swoon," which "became for him an image of the soul in prayer, humiliated and faint before her Creator" (P, 150); sacred art provides the emotional model he will emulate. Although he engages in great mortification of the senses, he demonstrates his impatience with the painstaking qualities of his lifestyle, feeling anger at his mother's sneezes and any other intrusion on his prayer. His final disaffection from devout practice results from a "sensation of spiritual dryness" and "period of desolation in which the sacraments themselves seemed to have turned into dried up sources" (P, 152). He finds surcease for this dark night of the spirit in the "imagery of the canticles," the wellspring of mystical inspiration. Much as in his youthful erotic fantasies, he imagines the surrender of the soul as a kind of marriage, opposed to the "voices of the flesh" that murmur through his head. He doubts his ability to continue his mended life, relying finally in all of his religiosity on love as the mystical concept that inspires goodness.

This theology of love supplants religion with art. When the director of the college asks whether Stephen has a vocation for the priesthood, their mutual joke about "les jupes" worn by the Capuchins arouses Stephen's reveries of old: "The names of articles of dress worn by women or of certain soft and delicate stuffs used in their making brought always to his mind a delicate and sinful perfume" (P, 155). Yet his fantasy is tempered by a perception of interior life that his former erotic imaginings did not possess: "it was only amid softworded phrases or within rosesoft stuffs that he dared to conceive of the soul or body of a woman moving with tender life" (P, 155). He imaginatively extends his thoughts to other people. While he may envision himself as a "young and silent-mannered priest," he only does so with the realization that the "awful power," "secret knowledge," and "obscure things" that he would know necessitate removal from others and allow only "a grave and ordered and passionless life . . . without material cares" (P, 160). And Stephen cares very greatly about passion, and materiality. The ritualistic life that he constructed around the "black cold void waste" of nothingness denied all human attributes in an effort to ascertain a God beyond comprehensibility. As he acknowledges, he "was destined to learn his own wisdom apart from others or to learn the wisdom of others himself wandering among the snares of the world." Those snares "were its ways of sin. He would fall . . . he felt the silent lapse of his soul . . . still unfallen but about to fall" (P, 162). The sin into which he falls emerges from the texture of his own memory, imagination, will, and circumstance; as he says, "he smiled to think that it was this disorder, the misrule of his father's house and the stagnation of vegetable life, which was to win the day in his soul" (P, 162). Disorder and misrule impose their own higher, sacred structure on Stephen's mind and enable the manufacture of image. Almost literally, for Stephen, love has pitched its mansion in the place of excrement.

This philosophy of love prompts Stephen's final rejection of the priesthood. His image of himself returning to the Church, a beggar asking for alms and loving forgiveness, battles against "his own dispassionate certitude, that the commandment of love bade us not to love our neighbor as ourselves with the same amount and intensity of love but to love him as ourselves with the same kind of love" (P, 166). Stephen rejects holy orders because his interpretation of love surpasses the outward form and practice required for religious adherence; in effect, while his subject remains secular, Stephen professes a religiosity of temperament more profoundly attuned to the contemplative thinking of the mystics than are the flat practice and pinched authority of the Church. His is a rebellion of spirit as much as of intellect. The radical challenge inherent in loving another with the same kind of love as one reserves for oneself requires mental liberation from the constraints of logic, misguided morality, and fear of incertitude, thus permitting an active engagement with life and a positive response to one's own subjectivity. When Stephen follows his pronouncement about love with the observation "A day of dappled seaborne clouds" (*P*, 166), he lifts uncertainty by its own metaphor, seeing in the reality of the clouds the heritage of centuries of mystical tracts on the happy impossibility of ever arriving at perfect knowledge, either of God or of one's own mind. As Gifford points out, the phrase originates in a nineteenth-century geology text that attempts to reconcile creationism with evolution. In the context of Stephen's mystical reading and meditation about love, the allusion suggests the perfect compromise between delight in one's subjectivity and mental processes and pleasure in transforming them into a connectedness with others—a bridge between his interior mental world and exterior reality. The transformation that occurs to Stephen, of course, is artistic. As he says:

The phrase and the day and the scene harmonized in a chord. Words. Was it their colours? He allowed them to glow and fade, hue after hue: sunrise gold, the russet and green of apple orchards, azure of waves, the greyfringed fleece of clouds. No, it was not their colours: it was the poise and balance of the period itself. Did he then love the rhythmic rise and fall of words better than their associations of legend and colour? Or was it that, being as weak of sight as he was shy of mind, he drew less pleasure from the reflection of the glowing sensible world through the prism of a language manycoloured and richly storied than from the contemplation of an inner world of individual emotions mirrored perfectly in a lucid supple periodic prose? (*P*, 166–67)

As usual, Stephen fuses senses, hearing the scenery and reflecting upon the color of the words; however, this meditation differs in his acknowledgment that his own disposition gears him toward "contemplation of an inner world" beyond the sensible, yet "mirrored" in the tangible form of writing. The sensibility is Paterian and suggests that, to Stephen, the creation of the text of his own mind, the representation of his own consciousness, becomes the most actual, sensual, and real of subjects.

This connection with the most actual of subjects makes possible the epiphany on the beach. As he approaches the ocean he has an experience of transcendence that takes the mystical transport of the soul as its model. He recollects the banter of his boyhood, dwells upon the mythical derivation of his name, and sees a "winged form" flying above the waves. Stephen, who interprets the world very much according to books, wonders about its significance: "What did it mean? Was it a quaint device opening a page of some medieval book of prophecies and symbols, a hawklike man flying sunward above the sea, a prophecy of the end he had been born to serve and had been following through the mists of childhood and boyhood, a symbol of the artist forging anew in his workshop out of the sluggish matter of the earth a new soaring impalpable imperishable being? . . . His heart trembled in an ecstasy of fear and his soul was in flight. His soul was soaring in an air beyond the world and the body he knew was purified in a breath and delivered of incertitude and made radiant and commingled with the element of the spirit" (*P,* 168–69). Stephen locates his origins in medieval culture and Neoplatonic philosophy. He suggests that the "sluggish matter of the earth" forms the subject of art, transmuted through the mental "workshop" of the artist. Despite the alchemical metaphor, the ecstasy of the body and mind achieves a mystical unity with untranscendent transcendence. Following this rapture he envisions himself resurrected, relinquishing the "cerements" of dull duty and ritual and able to respond to the vision of the girl on the beach whose "mortal beauty" inspires his cry of "Heavenly God" and furnishes him with the beginning of his artistic liturgy, the "advent of the life that had cried to him." He announces the creed of his new life after "her image had passed into his soul forever." He vows to "live, to err, to fall, to triumph, to recreate life out of life" through the worship of "the angel of mortal youth and beauty" who "open[ed] before him in an instant of ecstasy the gates of all the ways of error and glory" (*P,* 172). This birth of the artist from the spirit of sensuality originates in the advent of subjectivity and the epiphany of personal revelation. The chapter closes with Stephen gazing toward the dusky horizon, evoking Pater's Conclusion to *The Renaissance* in his observation of the rising tide that surrounds the "last few figures in distant pools."

Stephen contextualizes his awareness of sensuality and subjectivity in the rebellion and subversive thought of his quest, to echo Yeats, to write the "sacred book" of Irish consciousness (Yeats, 187). He imagines himself born of the Middle Ages—"His mind, in the vesture of a doubting monk, stood often in the shadow under the windows of that age" (*P,* 176)—seeing his mind as religiously inspired and noting that intellectual clarity arrives as a kind of enlightenment through obscurity. He records the process of enlightenment as revelation through language and image, recollecting the face of Cranly as that of a "guilty priest" through whose image "he had a glimpse of a strange dark cavern of speculation." From this image of the indeterminate nature of speculation emerges a sensitivity to the nuance and quality of words such that "every mean shop legend bound his mind like the words of a spell and his soul shrivelled up, sighing with age as he walked on in a lane among heaps of dead language. His own consciousness of language was ebbing from his brain and trickling into the very words themselves which set to band and disband themselves in wayward rhythm" (*P*, 179). Stephen articulates language as a sensory, rhythmic medium that possesses a life of its own and merges with his interior thoughts much like the actual debris of the Dublin streets that he walks. Through this mental cavern he imagines his position relative to learning as that of "a shy guest at the feast of the world's culture" whose "monkish learning, in terms of which he was striving to forge out an esthetic philosophy, was held no higher by the age he lived in than the subtle and curious jargons of heraldry and falconry" (*P*, 180).

Stephen dwells upon the speculative nature of his consciousness. When Davin narrates his evocative encounter with the peasant woman in her cottage, Stephen thinks to himself that the erotic allure of her "batlike soul waking to the consciousness of itself in darkness and secrecy and loneliness" (*P*, 183) is far more poetic than his ideas about "esthetic intellection," despite their congruence with medieval habits of apprehension. In other words, Davin's encounter captures more profoundly the appeal to the eye and mind of the "darkness and secrecy" of speculation than does the glimpse from the cliffs of Mohor "into the depths" offered by the dean. In the same manner, the joke offered by Stephen's friend during math class about "ellipsoidal balls" rushes "like a gust through the cloister of Stephen's mind, shaking into gay life limp priestly vestments that hung upon the walls, setting them to sway and caper in a sabbath of misrule" (*P*, 192). Stephen relates his friend's humor to the playful irreverence of the sabbath of misrule, or the revels of the boy bishop on Holy Innocents' Day, 28 December. The feast, especially popular in France, Germany, and England, traces to the tenth century, although it survived well into the fifteenth in England. The tradition consists of ensconcing choirboys in senior clergy positions and electing a boy bishop, all of whom are attired in priestly garb. The feast is especially relevant in the context of the college and, of course, in the satirical yet vested relationship that Stephen maintains with the Church. In this instance Stephen acknowledges the primacy of misrule or creative chaos in his makeup, its origin in medieval religious culture, and its relevance, whether through humor or sensuality, to the construction of speculative consciousness.

Stephen manipulates conversations with his friends as an occasion to act out his own intellectual misrule, subversion of authority, and artistic birth. He tells Davin that the soul "has a slow and dark birth, more mysterious than the birth of the body," to which his pragmatic Irish nationalist friend replies, "Too deep for me, Stevie . . . you can be a poet or a mystic after" (*P*, 203). Stephen reacts by denying patriotism and continuing his disquisition on Aristotle, concluding that the difficulties of artistic representation emerge from the fact that "we are just now in a mental world" whose divisions we must overcome in "the act itself of esthetic apprehension" (*P*, 208). Apprehension itself is the cornerstone of Stephen's artistic metaphysic; however, this "applied Aquinas," as he calls it, fails to communicate "artistic conception, artistic gestation and artistic reproduction" (*P*, 209). This vocabulary of reproduction links advent with the incarnation, thus reconciling the heritage of mystical devotion with the world of everyday appearance and observation. Christ becomes a god with attributes, emerging from the void of nothingness and taking sensible form. Art emerges from sensation and perception and fills the void of consciousness.

This cycle of apprehension and creation forms the spatial and temporal qualities of the art object that allow its perception as distinct from other objects: the "esthetic image is first luminously apprehended as selfbounded and selfcontained upon the immeasurable background of space or time which is not." To Stephen sensory perception is nothing short of transcendent, and he rhapsodically describes the instant "wherein that . . . clear radiance of the esthetic image is apprehended luminously by the mind which has been arrested by its wholeness . . . a spiritual state . . . called the enchantment of the heart" (*P*, 213). The literature of divine union favors the metaphor of the heart as the emblem of Christ's love as well as his humanity. Stephen emphasizes the human dimension of his theory with a metaphor of film and director: "The personality of the artist, at first a cry or a cadence or a mood and then a fluid and lambent narrative, finally refines itself out of existence, impersonalises itself, so to speak. The esthetic image in the dramatic form is life purified in and reprojected from the human imagination. The mystery of esthetic like that of material creation is accomplished. The artist, like the God of the creation, remains within or behind or beyond or above his handiwork, invisible, refined out of existence, indifferent, paring his fingernails" (*P*, 215). Stephen's model of God as artist, refined out of existence, exactly matches the incomprehensible God of Dionysius' *Divine Names*, whose absence constitutes his essence. Stephen's model of artistic creation is that of the contemplative who seeks no image, yet must accommodate the divine in human, tangible, and sensual form.

The penultimate section of chapter 5 turns to this human, tangible, and sensual form most fully. Fresh from his dream and composition of the villanelle, Stephen locates in the "enchantment of the heart" his "morning knowledge" (*P*, 213). This knowledge emerges from the tradition of mystical literature: "The instant flashed forth like a point of light and now from cloud on cloud of vague circumstance confused form was veiling softly its afterglow. O! in the virgin womb of the imagination the word was made flesh. Gabriel the seraph had come to the virgin's chamber. An afterglow deepened within his spirit, whence the white flame had passed, deepening to a rose and ardent light" (*P*, 217). The moment of artistic inspiration follows the pattern of divine union, expressed here, as in its parent literature, as light piercing the clouds. Mary, long the object of Stephen's devotion, personifies the imagination in the pattern of the annunciation, and representation in the birth and gestation of Christ. The light suffuses with its "roselike glow" the rhythm and rhyme of language, whose incantatory power is like "incense ascending from the altar of the world" (*P*, 218). The passage climaxes in a melding of the image of the world from his boyhood geography book, the incense column sent up by his devout prayers, and the ellipsoidal balls of his intellectual rebellion in college: "The earth was like a swinging smoking swaying censer, a ball of incense, an ellipsoidal ball" (*P*, 218). The image breaks and he hastily scribbles out his poem, fearful of forgetting it. He looks up, displeased with his unrequited love, and is "confounded by the print of the Sacred Heart above the untenanted sideboard" (*P*, 219). The devotion to the Sacred Heart has its origins in the early Middle Ages and probably began as a way of commemorating the waters from the rock that Moses struck, which prefigures Christ as the fountainhead of the Holy Spirit. The devotion was a favorite among medieval mystics as an expression of subjective piety. Its imagery and ritual are reflected in the writings of Bernard of Clairvaux, Bonaventure, and the commentaries on the Song of Songs. The Jesuits particularly adopted the devotion, although Saint Margaret Mary Alacoque popularized the observance in the seventeenth century. The heart venerates both "the physical heart and total love of Christ," thus symbolizing "twofold spiritual love, human and divine" (*NCE*, 820). The devotion consisted of enthroning the heart in the home and living one's daily life more aligned with Christ and Mary. Stephen quite clearly imagines his poetry as devotion to the Sacred Heart, whose observance requires the meditation on the nature and kind of love that he has earlier located in the embrace of life itself. The devotion renders him, a few pages later, "a priest of the eternal imagination, transmuting the daily bread of experience into the radiant body of everliving life" (*P*, 221). Experience and imagination become the host of life, and Stephen imagines a "roseway" from the flowers on the tattered wallpaper that leads to heaven. His amalgamation of art, inspiration, and theology leads him finally to transform his estrangement with Emma into an image of holy and sexual union. In the "mysterious ways of spiritual life" he becomes mentally "enfolded" in her nakedness, "radiant, warm, odorous and lavishlimbed." The product of his passive reproductive union is "the liquid letters of speech, symbols of the element of mystery" that comprise his poem. Artistic gestation is passive spiritual union, sex in the head. It is also sex in the flesh, active engagement with sensual life.

The book concludes, appropriately, with the most autobiographical of spiritual and literary forms, the diary. From the stuff of his everyday life Stephen strives for untranscendent transcendence. Before the diary entries begin he remarks that "reproduction is the beginning of death," thus connecting artistic gestation with mortality, absence, and obscurity as the matrix of art and existence. While he shocks Cranly with his rejection of the Church and his reluctance either to believe or to disbelieve in God, he does retain a mind "supersaturated with the religion" from which he desists. Stephen has left the Church through "the backdoor of sin" but finds his being and becoming in a secularized holiness. In the 5 April diary entry he writes, "Wild spring. Scudding clouds. O life!" The cloud motif continues in the diary, as does the model of artistic reproduction from the stuff of life. In the 6 April entry he invokes Michael Robartes in recollection of Yeats's idiosyncratic mysticism and wish to create a "sacred book" of aesthetics: "I desire to press in my arms the loveliness which has not yet come into the world." The final lines—"Welcome, O life! I go to encounter for the millionth time the reality of experience and to forge in the smithy of my soul the uncreated conscience of my race . . . Old father, old artificer, stand me now and ever in good stead"—expand time and defy ordinary limits to figure Stephen as the forger of his own reality, father of his consciousness, and, in his artifice, son and heir to his own intellectual heritage.

Portrait thus presents the ambiguities of the visual imagination in an exploration of memory, will, and understanding, concepts central to the negative mystical tradition and to the intellectual context of the novel. Stephen's manifesto transforms the language of religious discourse into a sensory, sensual revelation of the mind to itself. In his pursuit of self-knowledge Stephen encounters the radically subjective nature of word and image and uses the religious vocabulary of the mind to describe the secular artistry of the body and articulate ultimate reality, his greatest act of obeisance in the vesture of a doubting monk.

4

Getting on Nicely in the Dark
Perception in *Ulysses*

In *Portrait* Joyce unites asceticism, aestheticism, and sexual experience to articulate the nature of art and knowledge according to a secularized model of mysticism. *Ulysses* continues the pursuit of thought and sensuality in the ordinary as well as the erotic. As the book of day consciousness *Ulysses* places its inhabitants, in the rhetoric of "Oxen of the Sun," between "prenativity and postmortemity" in bonds of love and death, thus affirming the positive relationship of mind and body, sexuality and perception, to the absence and darkness of the "tenebrosity of the interior." This investigation of interior life corresponds to the traditional mystic search for the divine, which occurs at the most intimate level of personality and yields at once profound self-knowledge and nothingness. *Ulysses* shapes enlightenment in terms of human realities such as death, thus posing questions of being, annihilation, and imagination equivalent to the more celestial inquiries of the negative mystical tradition. Stephen, Bloom, and Molly in their own ways conflate the actuality and potentiality of human experience, reconciling in the novel's Jewish and Christian intellectual heritage the absence of knowledge with the presence of human compassion and creativity.

In "Ithaca" Stephen and Bloom's "artistic" and "scientific" temperaments work by a coincidence of opposites to shape the book's pursuit of knowledge in its reconciliation of sense and cognition. The chapter's catechistic questions unite the mundane to the metaphysical, suggestively reconciling the phenomenal and the ineffable world through the tradition of mysticism, the "science" that supersedes the more orthodox science governing the chapter. "Ithaca" culminates the teleology of the mind developed in earlier chapters; specifically, its intellectual discussion of Maimonides reveals why Stephen's "mystical finesse . . . [was] a bit out of [Bloom's] sublunary depth" (*U*, 629). In his reply to a question about "postexilic eminence" Bloom postulates "Three seekers of the pure truth, Moses of Egypt, Moses Maimonides, author of *More Nebukim* (Guide for the Perplexed) and Moses Mendelssohn of such eminence that from Moses (of Egypt) to Moses there arose none like Moses (Maimonides)" (*U*, 563). Maimonides ranks as the supreme medieval Jewish authority on Aristotle, and the mention of his most important text, the *Guide for the Perplexed,* serves ironically to comment on the spiritual state of Bloom's "scientific"—and Jewish—disposition. Maimonides wrote the *Guide* to synthesize the teaching of Aristotle with the doctrine of Judaism, thus shaping medieval debates over the status of the mind and senses. Although not mystical, the work of this "seeker of the pure truth" particularly elucidates the relationship of mysticism to rationalism, absence to knowledge, Stephen to Bloom.

Maimonides presents his *Guide* "to thinkers whose studies have brought them into collision with religion" and to those who "while firm in religious matters, are perplexed and bewildered on account of the ambiguous and figurative expressions employed in the holy writings" (Maimonides, 9). To those who doubt traditional images of God and explanations of the origin and eternity of the universe, the *Guide* addresses fifty-four chapters that explore the tension between revealed faith and intellectual philosophy. In *Ulysses* Bloom represents the rationalist who philosophizes his existence in terms of the imagination, and a few of the *Guide*'s central debates turn away from philosophy to the possibility of a creative universe. A brief description of its propositions about the attributes of God, matter, the imagination, and *creatio ex nihilo* in the context of medieval Jewish thought about sexuality illuminates its connection with the intellectual debates of mysticism and *Ulysses* construction of a sensualized aesthetic.

In essence Maimonides follows the tradition of medieval Jewish thought, which distrusts matter as the origin of pleasure, yet must reconcile asceticism with the necessity of marriage and sexuality (Biale, 92). Maimonides considers the problem of representation, in which God transcends time, space, and materiality. He thus asks "whether some real relationship exists between God and any of the substances created by Him, by which he could be described" (Maimonides, 71)? The answer is no because of the impossibility of accidents that would furnish positive attributes. As a result, for Maimonides, "the negative attributes of God are the true attributes . . . on the one hand they do not imply any plurality, and, on the other, they convey to man the highest possible knowledge of God" (Maimonides, 81–82). In other words, one's relationship to God, and hence to all knowledge, must rest on proof of the unprovable, so that "every time you establish by proof the negation of a thing in reference to God, you become more perfect, while with every additional positive assertion you follow your imagination and recede from the true knowledge of God" (Maimonides, 84). Naturally this apophatic view of God and knowledge subsumes mental and physical realities to philosophy and resembles Christian mysticism's fundamental impasse of understanding, which necessarily divides creator from created.

This impasse points to a preoccupation with the imagination and senses. Against the orthodox meaning of the imagination, which proposes that "the test for the possibility of an imagined object does not consist in its conformity with the existing laws of nature" (Maimonides, 120), Maimonides argues that it is impossible to assume imagined circumstances. He considers it impossible, for example, to imagine that a beast or man should be of an unnatural size, or that "an accident should become a substance, or that one substance should penetrate another" (Maimonides, 128). In this manner he refutes the possibility of a universe created by imagination, stating directly that reason discerns humans from animals, who do possess imagination. The primacy of intellect over the imagination, Maimonides states, allows the perception of the world as it truly is; all else is "fiction, a phantasm . . . Nor can imagination in any way obtain a purely immaterial image of an object, however abstract the form of the image may be. Imagination yields therefore no test for the reality of a thing" (Maimonides, 130). Against this view of the imagination Aquinas will later propose that the soul understands nothing without a phantasm and fuel Stephen and Bloom's relentless desire to know whether the artistic imagination may test for reality, or whether there is indeed any reality beyond their mental construction.

For Maimonides the reality beyond the purely mental lies in the proofs of the existence of God and of the creation of the universe from nothing. Among the various propositions that begin his proof of creation, he considers the nature of motion, which presupposes change and transition from potentiality to actuality. Motion, specifically causing shifts in place but generally any change, supplies one of the central arguments for the creation of the universe, in which time and space function as its accidents and bring things into actuality. In this philosophy, the existence of things supports the validity of Scripture, which allows for the incorporeal, uncreated God to create a mutable world.

This mutability allows for religion, through which, "accepting the Creation, we find that miracles are possible, that Revelation is possible" (Maimonides, 199). Averroes, whose writings influenced Maimonides, responds to the rationalistic denial of revealed faith that prevailed in the Islam of his day. In his work *Tahafut al-Tahafut* (The Incoherence of the Incoherence) he reconciles faith in reason with the mysteries of creation. Maimonides addresses creation as a rationalistic philosopher by reconciling the glories of the intellect with religious enlightenment and ascribes to faith what in the secular domain belongs to the subjective creativity of the artist. Yet in this rendering of potentiality into actuality, the question remains, "was that only possible which came to pass?" (*U*, 21).

Against "Averroes and Moses Maimonides, dark men in mein and movement," other medieval Jewish thinkers resisted Maimonidean actuality in favor of the mystical traditions of Kabbalah, the better to comprehend the "darkness shining in brightness" of absence, negation, and sexual creativity (*U*, 23). Writing generally of the Jewish mystical tradition, Gershom Scholem states that "there is no room for mysticism so long as the abyss between Man and God has not become a fact of inner consciousness" (*Major Trends*, 7). The desire for God arises from a perception of utter absence and abandonment, cosmic in proportion. The mystic's fundamental impulse is to fulfill that desire for God, to apprehend and potentially attain divine union at the end of what Scholem calls the "quest for the secret that will close it [divine apprehension] in" (*Major Trends*, 8). In asking who God is and how the mind knows, the mystic comes up against the intractable paradox of how one can know, much less represent, what is by definition beyond comprehension, outside of human dimension. Scholem observes that the mystic resolves this paradox by envisioning the personal God in the apophatic God of Kabbalah, in "the depths of His nothingness" (*Major Trends*, 12). Kabbalah thus presents an interesting solution to the problem of materiality. *Ein-Sof,* its deepest principle of infinity, resists any form or shape. In Scholem's words, "It is beyond any cognitive statements, and can only be described through negation—indeed, as the negation of all negation. No images can depict it, nor can it be named by any name" (*Godhead,* 38). Closely paralleling the diction and thought of Dionysius the Areopagite's *Divine Names,* the kabbalistic infinite principle of hidden divinity also takes active form in symbols, thus reinscribing the paradox of representation characterized by its Christian counterpart. This conceptual and imagistic God is both male and female and finds its most profound Kabbalistic expression in literal and figurative sexual union, reconciling the division of body and soul by equating the concept of secrecy with the attainment of sexual knowledge. John of the Cross's diagram of the ascent of the mount that culminates in *nada* suggestively repeats this model and raises questions of shared Iberian roots, on the hill of Howth as well as in the gardens of the Alameda.

"Proteus" explores this relation between the creative imagination and the senses by conceptualizing aesthetics as the search for beauty amid apophasis. In *Portrait* Stephen immerses his mind in theological pattern and practice in order to forge his artistic consciousness; in *Ulysses* he extends this novitiate to the exploration of epistemological uncertainty against the certainties of Scholasticism and the mysteries of the body. The tropological structure of the chapter set in the context of George Berkeley's philosophy and Jacob Boehme's theology establishes Stephen's curiosity about mystical thought as his way of exploring the nature of manifestation, both human and divine. *Ulysses* begins by invoking the *Introit* of the Mass, the moment in the liturgy which traditionally introduces its theme through musical or other embellishment. The development of the Mass occasioned the use of tropes, introduced during the Introit, which commented, explained, or reinforced the object of the service. In "Proteus" the quest for the nature of knowing and moment of creative enlightenment resembles the search for surety embraced in the motif of the *quem queritis*. The trope originated in Psalm 138, "quem queritis in sepulchro," and developed a Christmas cycle complement, "quem queritis in presepe." The answer at the tomb is *non est hic*; at the manger, *adest hic* (Young, 223). *Ulysses*, the book of "yes," inclines toward the union of father and son, mind and enlightenment, through a long day of seeking out the essence of understanding and creation. Much as "light to the gentiles" Bloom fulfills the promise of the Christmas cycle, so too Stephen inaugurates the search for metaphysical, hence aesthetic, manifestation. He must reconcile himself to the nature of absence, the tomb of his mother's death, if he wishes to glimpse the possibility of creativity in its shadow. In "Proteus" Stephen deliberately shuts out the day of rational comprehensibility in order to examine the nature of being through literal and spiritual darkness, in order to say of family, society, and book learning that "beauty is not there" but rather in the approach *ad altare mentis*.

As a disaffected medical student, exile, and confirmed solipsist, Stephen embodies his implied nickname. Referring to his behavior at his mother's deathbed, Mulligan says, "You could have knelt down, damn it, Kinch, when your dying mother asked you . . . I'm hyperborean as much as you" (*U*, 5). Emanuel Swedenborg, scientist and mystic, began the Society of Sciences of Uppsala's first scientific journal, entitled "Daedaelus Hyperboreus." Although the *Arcana Coelestia* is his most compendious work, it is his later *Soul-Body Interaction* that describes the correspondences between various parts of the body and spiritual attributes or rewards in heaven. This correlation of person to universe nicely resonates with *Ulysses'* chapter organization around bodily organs. Appropriately "Proteus" lacks any physical correlative in the scheme of the book, positioning the inquiry of Stephen, the Dedalus Hyperborean, between doubt of scientific positivism and faith in religious insubstantiality, a position that undermines simple belief in the autonomy of the subject through its questioning of the status of the senses.

The first paragraph announces Stephen's preoccupation with the tension between Aristotelian apprehension, "thought through my eyes," and the supersensual character of the sensory. While pondering the limitations of the "ineluctable modality of the visible," which establishes space as determined by physical bodies, he invokes both Berkeley and Boehme to explain the untranscendent transcendence of art. Berkeley advocated immaterialism as the philosophy that expressed the relationship of subjectivism and epistemological realism. In so doing he reacted against scientific positivism, suggesting, for example, the absurdity of belief in physics as the determiner of reality. Gifford notes that Stephen thinks of "snotgreen, bluesilver, rust" as "coloured signs," thus echoing Berkeley's concept in *An Essay towards a New Theory of Vision* of the relative, discrete impression that each sense perceives which acts in concert with impressions of other senses to form the shape of a thing. The contours of "Proteus" invite a closer reading of Berkeley's philosophy of the mind; there is more than meets the eye. In the *New Theory* he analyzes sight as the ability to perceive not only the exterior form of objects but also the design of God in their meaning. Things exist in the relativism of the mind but nonetheless signify "divine visual language." Although Berkeley acknowledges the subjective nature of apprehension, things do depend on awareness for existence; there is reciprocity between perceiver and perceived. People and sensible creatures therefore require suspension in mental awareness, leading him to suggest that "there must be some other mind wherein they exist." This "other mind" in which objects and perception exist perhaps constitutes the focus of Stephen's search in "Proteus": the possibility of a presence beyond and around him that defines his awareness. In asking the question "Am I walking into eternity along Sandymount strand?" Stephen forms his own answer by "getting on nicely in the dark." With his eyes closed he assures himself of concrete materiality by tapping his cane and hearing the crack of seashells under his feet. But when he opens his eyes he confirms not so much the independence of objects from human awareness as their radical contingency: "See now. There all the time without you: and ever shall be, world without end." Although he reassures himself that they were "there all the time," the invocation of the Gloria asserts the presence of the divine in a never-changing relationship with human intellect and sensory perception, a "world without end." The "signatures of all things" that he reads not only reflect the spiritual vision of its source, Boehme, but also resonate with Stephen's exploration of his presence in space, "what you damned well have to see" if you presume to exist. To Stephen the artist, perplexed by his own doubt of the "other mind" of his existence, the imagination must indeed test for the reality of the thing.

While Stephen shapes his ontological experiment partly in response to Berkeley's philosophy, the "signatures of all things" that he is there to read directly alludes to the writings of Jacob Boehme and his mystical framing of the artistic imagination. Michael Patrick Gillespie notes that Joyce owned the 1912 Everyman edition of Boehme in his Trieste library, entitled *The Signature of All Things, With Other Writings.* The book contains three treatises: "Signatura Rerum," "Of Supersensual Life," and "The Way from Darkness to True Illumination." The titles suggest appropriate categories within which to construe Stephen's search for divine and personal manifestation in the flotsam of the beach. Clifford Bax furnished the introduction to the volume, and his remarks indicate precisely the transcendence from ordinary consciousness that Stephen attempts.[1] Stating floridly that "mysticism is the romance of religion," he declares that "it is either the noblest folly or the grandest achievement of man's mind . . . The purpose of the mystic is the mightiest and most solemn that can ever be, for the central aim of all mysticism is to soar out of separate personality up to the very consciousness of God" (Boehme, ix). No introductory remark more precisely echoes the mentality of Stephen in *Portrait*, whose daedalian flight from "nationality and religion" leads him at once to consider the limits of consciousness.

Boehme's words establish the direction of Stephen's mental excursion, which seeks correspondence between the physical reality of the beach and the order of mystery it reveals. According to Boehme spiritual inquiry consists of "seeking and finding" in the absence of will and desire. In this state of passivity one may begin to approach what he terms "the grand mystery of all beings," only possible if one strives to "understand the nothing, for without nature is the nothing" (Boehme,

22). The presence of nothing paradoxically exists within the contour of the mind because the "whole outward visible world" emblemizes the "signature of the inward, spiritual" (Boehme, 91). Stephen yokes Berkeley's "other mind" with the search for revealed absence to refine his protean inquiry into the aesthetic origin of things as a quest for beauty amid apophasis. If in Boehme's language the "creation of the whole creation is nothing else but a manifestation of the all-essential, unsearchable God" (Boehme, 210), then Stephen's aesthetics marry a flawed awareness of flesh with a perfect consciousness of doubt.

After Stephen establishes the contingent nature of the "world without end," he observes two slatternly women, maybe midwives, whose "sisterhood" brought him "squealing into life." Their presence inspires a meditation upon birth as "creation from nothing" in which all people umbilically link back to Eden. He then explains to himself: "That is why mystic monks. Will you be as gods? Gaze in your *omphalos*" (*U*, 32). The *omphalos* of their attention is certainly figural, the introspective navel-gazing of the nineteenth-century aesthetic preoccupation with perception; after all, Stephen does think of himself "like Algy," seeing in the sea the mother of all life. But he also imagines his conception, suggesting that the mystical purview of the monks extends quite literally to the origin in which he was "wombed in sin darkness," divinely willed into being and incapable of ever being willed away. This meditation upon suspension in uterine darkness and divine "lex eterna" prompts him to wonder whether his immutability is itself "the divine substance wherein Father and Son are consubstantial" (*U*, 32), a coexistence that suggests to him that the introspective, omphalic gaze coincides with the deity's will to comprise reality.

As Stephen the fatherless son seeks affirmation in the texture of reality, his gaze turns inward toward spiritual failure: "you will never be a saint. Isle of saints" (*U*, 34). He recalls the obsessive devotions of his youth chronicled in *Portrait* and invokes Ireland's epithet, "isle of saints and sages," in an ironic dismissal of his spiritual shortcomings as typical of his nation's lassitude. While in this self-deprecating mode Stephen assaults the essence of traditional manifestation itself, the moment of epiphany, by recollecting his "epiphanies written on green oval leaves, deeply deep" (*U*, 34). Having undermined the notion of privileged revelation as the summit of experience, he confronts the reality of the strand, "damp crackling mast, razorshells, squeaking pebbles" which literally texture the sand. As he walks, the beach metamorphoses into "sewage breath, a pocket of seaweed smouldered in seafire under a midden of man's ashes." Amid the bleak rubble he observes "a porterbottle . . . sogged to its waist, in the cakey sand dough." Stephen perceives the bottle as "a sentinel: isle of dreadful thirst," at once recalling the "isle of saints" and suggesting "The City of Dreadful Night." Like the bottle on the beach that signifies thirst amid squalor, Thomson's poem focuses on spiritual desolation as the fundamental state of modern consciousness. This moment of recognition constitutes its own sort of revelation, and Stephen's view brings the sentinel post of the bottle into perspective: "Broken hoops on the shore; at the land a maze of dark cunning nets; farther away chalkscrawled backdoors and on the higher beach a dryingline with two crucified shirts" (U, 34). The "dark cunning nets" recall the constraints of nationality and religion from which the young Stephen fled, yet here foreground a scene of Irish domesticity laden with epiphanic potential. The "chalkscrawled backdoors" faintly recollect the feast of the Epiphany itself, whose ancient celebration included the marking of doors with chalk.[2] In this same panorama the "two crucified shirts" innocently posing as laundry naturally evoke the image of Calvary but with a missing third person, in keeping with Stephen's overall deflation of the promise of salvation. The absence of Christ provokes a moment of introspective anti-enlightenment in which Stephen observes in the premise of redemption the fullness of abjection; he sees in the "human shells" of the beach's economy the empty signature of all things.

The failed search for revealed meaning in the casual features of the strand prompts Stephen to wonder at the design of his own nature. Stepping in the wet sand he envisions the tower where he will not sleep, anticipating "Ithaca's" lonely yet alluring "nightblue" in the "blue dusk, nightfall, deep blue night" of the tower's alienation. In an act of rejection he declares, "Take all, keep all. My soul walks with me, form of forms" (U, 37), locating within himself the Platonic origin of his physical and metaphysical drives. From this point of origin, much like the Ithacan final moment, his meditation proceeds. Spying "a point" on the horizon, Stephen fixes his gaze until it becomes a dog, *un chien bien visible*. The tradition of reading "dog" for God in Joyce criticism is well established; however, here the point of the point lies in the pattern of search and discovery that dominates Stephen's walk rather than in any identification with the divine. After all, Stephen's design is not so much confirmation of belief as reassurance of doubt. Nevertheless, the dog inspires fear, and Stephen worries, much like the speaker of Thompson's "Hound of Heaven," that he will be overcome by its presence. The concept of a sacred chase, of God seeking out an unwilling subject for his favors, recurs throughout the tradition of mystical literature.

In "Proteus" it laces Stephen's imagination and shows itself in his pre-occupation not only with the dog but also more generally with companionship and loneliness. Although the dog does not follow, Stephen nonetheless practices a kind of mental elusiveness in which he looks beyond the object of his fear in order to focus upon the nature of his own understanding. While he here walks in the company of his "soul," his attention focuses upon "figures, two. The two maries." Presumably the same two women who prompted his recollection of "creation from nothing," these "maries" similarly establish the theological vocabulary of the chapter, recalling of course the Marys at the tomb of the original *quem queritis*. Earlier Stephen imagines that the "maries" carried in their bag "a misbirth with a trailing navelcord" (*U*, 32); here "they have tucked it safe mong the bulrushes," thus conflating the concealment of Moses with the "allwombing tomb" (*U*, 40) of death and regeneration. The empty tomb suspends the question of presence in the matter of visual perception and being; Stephen's game of "peekaboo. I see you" that immediately follows establishes him at once as dodging the hand of God and desiring its hold. His disappointed "no, the dog" suggests that the pursuit mutually fails. As the last sentence of the paragraph wonders "who?" so too Stephen seeks the epiphanic God of creative manifestation to assure himself of existence. Like Moses to whom God appears in obscure form, Stephen figures himself as chosen for profound revelation; however, it is of the muddied, mortal, artistic kind.

Stephen continues to construct himself in terms of his anxiety about the dog: "Dog of my enemy. I just simply stood pale, silent, bayed about. *Terribilia meditans*" (*U*, 38). His terrible thoughts, unsurprisingly, follow the preoccupations of the day—his mother's death, drowning—and find their correlative in the actions of the dog, which recalls "Nestor's" inquiry into personality and being in terms of the riddle of the fox burying his own grandmother. In "Nestor" Stephen reforms the riddle to transpose guilt at his mother's death to a sense of his own spiritual doom. The fox, "red reek of rapine in his fur" (*U*, 23), scrapes the earth in search of his sin, the buried corpse, and Stephen furnishes this mental picture against the ruckus of hockeysticks and boys' voices outside the classroom. Later in the chapter the ignorantly nationalistic Deasy tells Stephen, "all human history moves toward one great goal, the manifestation of God." Stephen, in reply, gestures out to the shouting voices and says, "that is God . . . a shout in the street" (*U*, 28). In "Proteus" the dog on the beach trots, "looking for something lost in a past life" (*U*, 38), only to find it in the corpse of another dog: "sniffling rapidly like a dog all over the dead dog's bedraggled fell. Dogskull, dogsniff, eyes on the ground, moves to one great goal" (*U*, 39). The great goal of Stephen's adventure lies ultimately in the obscurity of self-perception; he must find in the relics of his own undoing the potential for psychological grace. He imagines the dog as the fox scratching in the sand for his grandmother, "dabbling, delving . . . vulturing the dead" (*U*, 39). Haunted by the sense that he sacrificed his mother upon the altar of his approach to individuality, Stephen is sandtrapped in the darkness of his *terribilia meditans*, vulturing the dead.

Stephen's need to reconcile death with art merges with the philosophy of Berkeley and Maimonides in his synthesis of the origins of the supersensual life. As his mind turns "to the west, trekking to evening lands" (*U*, 40), he perceives, if not accepts, physical and epistemological darkness as the positive source of aesthetic inspiration. In the "Nestor" passage that follows the vision of the fox, Stephen meditates upon "Averroes and Moses Maimonides, dark men in mien and movement, flashing in their mocking mirrors the obscure soul of the world, a darkness shining in brightness which brightness could not comprehend" (*U*, 23), to note the union of Aristotelian philosophy with metaphysical inquiry that typifies his sense of identity. In "Proteus" Stephen mouths sensuous kisses in the air, scribbles words on paper, and considers the stretch of his shadow on the rocks. About its length he wonders, "why not endless till the farthest star" (*U*, 40), thus echoing Berkeley's objection to the idea of geometrical limits to perception. He next thinks of the stars: "Darkly they are there behind this light, darkness shining in the brightness, delta of Cassiopeia, worlds" (*U*, 40). In resurrecting his earlier train of thought Stephen conjures what in "Nestor" comprises the essence of negative knowledge, the sense of meaning embedded in obscurity. Stephen considers whether he controls his shadow, his physical manifestation, through the agency of his imagination: "I throw this ended shadow from me, manshape ineluctable, call it back. Endless, would it be mine, form of my form?" In so doing he questions not only if imagination may serve to test for the reality of the thing, but also whether that reality is not utterly reliant on his consciousness, or another's. As he says, "Who watches me here?" thus invoking Berkeley's concept of human reality held within the mind of God. In a double-edged question he considers, "Who ever anywhere will read these written words?"—at once evoking the alienation of the artist and reinstating the larger mystery of the ultimate reader of the words of life whose "language tide and wind have silted here" (*U*, 37). In answer to his questions he again recalls Berkeley, the "good bishop of Cloyne," who "took the veil of the temple out of his shovel hat" (*U*, 40). As Gifford notes, the veil screens the holy of holies in the book of Exodus, "rent at the moment of Jesus' death." This too is the veil of Berkeley's visible world, whose signs are "the language of the Author of nature" (Berkeley, 231). However, the idea of a tear in the shroud of mystery suggests a shift in sensibility from a God without creation to one within its fold, capable of death. In other words, the design of God's language known only in the head nonetheless finds inscription only in the body. So Stephen says: "Darkness is in our souls don't you think?" swiftly locating consciousness within a paradigm of spiritual understanding through obscurity. He then proceeds to a brief scene of lovemaking, "a woman to her lover clinging, the more the more" (*U*, 40). Despite his disdain for the physical, it is in the "ineluctable modality of the ineluctable visuality" (*U*, 40) that Stephen locates the essence of self-inscription and release, which renders sexuality the ultimate expression of the supersensual life.

Action does not necessarily follow insight. Stephen considers his flirtation with "the virgin at Hodges Figgis' window" as well as his own potential homosexuality, "Wilde's love that dare not speak its name," but typically pursues neither fantasy; as in Berkeley's metaphysics, what is seen differs from what is touched. Instead he conflates the mortal with the morbid, urinating from the "Cock lake" into the "full fathoms out there," hoping to understand if not sex, death. His moment of tempered insight follows the revelation that in the cycle of existence he perceives, and therefore is, through his own and others' sensibility, so that "God becomes man becomes fish becomes barnacle goose becomes featherbed mountain. Dead breaths I living breathe, tread dead dust, devour a urinous offal from the dead" (*U*, 42). In this "world without end," Stephen arrives at the closest point in his search for the location of beauty. Figuring himself as Christ—"Come. I thirst. Clouding over . . . To evening lands. Evening will find itself" (*U*, 42)—he reconstructs the pattern of theological inquiry as the way from darkness to true illumination, but one which, to him, occurs in theory rather than in practice. At once pursuing and relinquishing his impulse toward ordered experience, he states that "evening will find itself in me, without me," thereby implying that inspiration occurs passively, without his assistance, outside his being. Against this dissolution of personality he verifies himself by assuming the Berkelian role of the author of the language of nature, placing his "dry snot picked from his nostril on a ledge of rock, carefully. For the rest let look who will" (*U*, 42). This act of physical graffiti, regressive yet transcendent like so many of Stephen's other bodily manifestos, directly precedes the chapter's moment of fulfillment—"Behind. Perhaps there is someone"—which completes the metaphysical "peekaboo" of his search with the implied response, *adest hic*. The cycle of artistic genesis is complete; Stephen contemplates the shift from the tomb of absence to the womb of presence, and recognizes, if not relishes, in his own flesh and being the sensate origins of knowledge. If the manifestation of God is a shout in the street, then the location of beauty, suspended in the mind of another and the realm of the senses, is his act of self-inscription upon the rock. The imagination has served to test for the reality of Stephen.

Bloom's construction of the visual imagination, as may be expected, unites the inquisitive mind and desiring body in positive confirmation of the link between the sensual world and cognition. His meditations, scattered in "Calypso," "Lotus-Eaters," and "Lestrygonians," frame consciousness between the bath and the frying pan in order to suggest that the body constructs the mind, simultaneously resisting and accepting the void of understanding. As the rational man who nonetheless grasps the more transcendent problems of unknowing, Bloom has unkosher thoughts of pork kidney breakfast and fleshy hips that stave off death by thought and touch, thus positioning physical decay and despair as part of the cycle of existence. He and Stephen define themselves against the premise of nullity as a means of testing not only the limits of their rational cognition but also the expanse of sense impression, but Bloom reconciles himself to the ordinary through its embrace, finding, for example, in the pattern of the Mass not Stephen's anxious inspiration but rather his own aesthetic of mortality.

Bloom consistently affirms the tension between a sacral and mortal universe and sees compassion in the human perspective. In "Calypso" he meditates upon farmland in the Middle East. His thoughts are obscured by a cloud that "cover[ed] the sun slowly, wholly. Grey. Far" (*U*, 50). The eclipse of light poses a challenge to Bloom's epistemology; after all, the morning began with "gelid light and air" diffusing the kitchen. His thoughts darken with the sky, and he reflects upon his earlier fruitful image of the farmland, declaring it to be "not like that" but instead "a barren land, bare waste. Vulcanic lake, the dead sea: no fish, weedless, sunk deep in the earth . . . Brimstone they called it raining down: the cities of the plain: Sodom, Gomorrah, Edom. All dead names. A dead sea in a dead land, grey and old. Old now. It bore the oldest, the first race" (*U*, 50). Bloom sees the origins of humanity traditionally in terms of Jewish myth and reproduction, figuring the land as "Dead: an old woman's: grey sunken cunt of the world" (*U*, 50). Bloom's

response to his insight—"Desolation. Grey horror seared his flesh"—
suggests that he reaches the nadir of his being, experienced physically
and mentally as utter despair of spirit.

As an alternative to the anxiety of death Bloom hastens toward home,
chased by "cold oils" and "crusting" age. As an antidote to time he
asserts his presence "now. Yes, I am here now" and disposes his mind
in homely contemplation of the coziness of "the gentle smoke of tea,
fume of the pan, sizzling butter. Be near her ample bedwarmed flesh.
Yes, yes" as the most immediate solution to the dark day. Having thus
calmed his immediate fear, he sees "Quick warm sunlight . . . running
from the Berkeley road, swiftly, in slim sandals, along the brightening
footpath. Runs, she runs to meet me, a girl with gold hair on the wind"
(U, 50). The flash of sun on the road suggests a young girl, maybe Milly,
who completes Bloom's meditation on death with a figure of youth.
Bloom sees in the sprightly figure of the sun the potential for imaginative transcendence. While Stephen reads in the signature of all things a
self-reflexive notion of artistry, Bloom necessarily reaches under the
covers and among his family to reassure himself of being. To Stephen
"God becomes man becomes fish becomes barnacle goose becomes
featherbed mountain. Dead breaths I living breathe" in a reluctant acceptance of the deterioration of the life cycle that determines his existence. In contrast, Bloom moves from abandonment to rejuvenation,
thus constructing in his visual language the pattern in which life becomes age becomes despair becomes the possibility of equanimity.

In "Lotus-Eaters" Bloom intensifies his vision of the death of the
body by contemplating the premise of the Mass and its relationship to
nothingness, absence, and nonbeing. He remarks upon the literal meaning of faith: "What? *Corpus:* body. Corpse . . . now I bet that makes them
feel happy. Lollipop. It does. Yes, bread of angels it's called. There's a
big idea behind it, kind of kingdom of God is within you feel. Then feel
all like one family party . . . Not so lonely" (U, 66). Bloom desires engagement with others in order to overcome his pervasive sense of alienation from Molly, Milly, Rudy, even the not-present Martha; to him the
value of faith lies in its ability to overcome separation through union,
literally rendered as food and cannibalism. Although he does not partake in the service, the words of the consecration diffuse Bloom's bath:
"clean trough of water, cool enamel, the gentle tepid stream. This is my
body" (U, 71). Like Stephen in "Proteus" he too imagines a uterine
state: "He foresaw his pale body reclined in it at full, naked, in a womb
of warmth, oiled by scented melting soap, softly laved"; however, unlike Stephen's "wombed in sin darkness," Bloom's vision is positively,

if passively, erotic, as is his vaguely expressed desire to masturbate in
the tub: "Also I think I. Yes I. Do it in the bath. Curious longing I. Water
to water. Combine business with pleasure" (*U*, 69). Finally, while Stephen gazes fearfully, testily, at the "omphalos" of origins, Bloom thinks
instead of the presence of sexuality, even if alone. He envisions his navel simply as the "bud of flesh" that blooms into the "languid floating
flower" of its beginnings, his penis. Bloom's visual language names the
body as the site of cognition and sexuality as the force through which
the mind's fuse reassures the flower of its being.

In "Lestrygonians" Bloom continues to test for the unity, not division, of his body and mind as a way of understanding the sensibility of
darkness. In his hungry mood the sensual pleasure of food dominates
his mental palate, and Elijah ben Bloom conflates the "Feast of Our
Lady of Mount Carmel" with "caramel" (*U*, 127), gently recalling the
Carmelite retreat from the things of the world in his quest for lunch. In
the same manner he wonders whether diet inclines one toward art, once
again quietly wondering at the relation between the senses and the
mind. "I wouldn't be surprised if it was that kind of food you see produces the like waves of the brain the poetical" (*U*, 136). The poetry of
his brainwaves moves lyrically toward the Middle East in conflation
of hunger, sensuality, and religion. He recalls Agendath Netaim, the
Zionist land investment scheme, which reminds him of the allure of
flesh so that "A warm human plumpness settled down on his brain.
His brain yielded. Perfume of embraces all him assailed. With hungered flesh obscurely, he mutely craved to adore" (*U*, 138). Gratification
comes at Davey Byrne's pub, where he savors his burgundy, seeing two
flies buzz on the windowpane and remembering from a "secret touch"
his first lovemaking with Molly: "Wildly I lay on her, kissed her: eyes,
her lips, her stretched neck beating, woman's breasts full in her blouse
of nun's veiling, fat nipples upright. Hot I tongued her. She kissed me.
I was kissed. All yielding she tossed my hair. Kissed, she kissed me"
(*U*, 144). Although he is indulging in a memory of passion, its resolution: "Me. And me now. Stuck, the flies buzzed" recalls the "desolation" of his crisis of age, which frightened him earlier in the morning.
Instead of reacting with horror, Bloom maintains his equanimity in the
face of change by putting Molly under a cloud of forgetting, instead
admiring the curve of the bar like the flank of a "shapely goddess." His
deflection of attention resembles a kind of emptying of the mind, suggesting that memory and sensation alone slake the drought of alienation and uncertainty.

At the chapter's close Bloom directly explores the role of visual language and its relation to the framing of consciousness. After watching the blind man avoid the van in the street he speculates in kindly sympathy that he "Must have felt it. See things in their forehead." His vision or understanding of the world, he thinks, must be "something blacker than the dark," and he remembers that the blind are called "dark men." Bloom, already a dark man in mein and movement, typically reconciles the potential for knowledge with the actual presence of the senses in his reordered vision of mind and body. He concludes that sex, "more shameless not seeing," must take place as a "form in his mind's eye. The voice, temperatures . . . passing over her white skin. Different feel perhaps. Feeling of white" (*U*, 149). Almost automatically Bloom tries to feel the color of his belly, the leading organ of the moment, in the manner of the blind man: "Walking by Doran's publichouse he slid his hand between his waistcoat and trousers and, pulling aside his shirt gently, felt a slack fold of his belly. But I know it's whitey yellow. Want to try in the dark to see." Echoing Stephen's attempt to get on without sight, Bloom too wants to know whether thought comes through the eyes, or mind, or both. His experiment deferred until the dark, Bloom thinks compassionately about the injustice of blindness and moves toward the affective expression that is his own bulwark against the "blacker than the dark" void. With hungered fingers darkly he obscurely craved to know.

While Bloom defines his artistic enterprise by taste and touch, Stephen in "Scylla and Charybdis" returns to the origins of creation, both artistic and personal, in nothing, in impalpability. In this chapter Stephen imagines the genesis of the artist and, in turn, postulates the ability to create as the central feature of the mind, which makes order from absence and chaos and thus unites the mind and the body. While the conversation in the library examines the contributions of esoteric thought to artistry, Stephen rejects the sophistry of theosophy in favor of his own sensibility, which sees the pattern of art and the form of identity in mysticism.

At the beginning of the chapter Eglington goads Stephen by asking about the "six brave medicals" who would write *Paradise Lost* at his behest, suggesting that "you would need one more for *Hamlet*. Seven is dear to the mystic mind" (*U*, 151). Thus the conversation about art and theology begins, squaring off Shakespeare's creativity against Stephen's anxiety over his public intellectual performance and private spiritual doubt. Almost immediately, the presence of A.E., George Russell, leading Dublin theosophist, emerges from the shadows of the room to pronounce the object of art, Shakespeare's or anyone else's, to be the revelation of "ideas, formless spiritual essences. The supreme question about a work of art is out of how deep a life does it spring . . . all the rest is the speculation of schoolboys for schoolboys" (*U*, 152). Stephen outwardly proclaims his Aristotelian sympathies against the insubstantial Platonism of Russell's credo by "superpolitely" suggesting that "the schoolmen were schoolboys first . . . Aristotle was once Plato's schoolboy" (*U*, 152). Privately he thinks of "Formless spiritual . . . Allfather, the heavenly man. Hiesos Kristos, magician of the beautiful, the Logos who suffers in us at every moment"; A.E.'s esoteric belief is incompatible with orthodox Christianity, and suits Stephen's need to undermine his relationship with God so that "this verily is that. I am the fire upon the altar. I am the sacrificial butter" (*U*, 152). Gifford has "sacrificial butter" as a conflation of Annie Besant's writing upon suffering and lines upon sacrifice from the *Bhagavadgita*. Stephen's object is the deflation of esoteric rhetoric to the absurd, suggesting his own desire to place in its stead his questionable faith in Aristotelian substantiality. His derision continues as he satirizes the claims to immortality made by the school of Madame Blavatsky, suggested by his recollection of "Mrs. Cooper Oakley" who "once glimpsed our very illustrious sister H.P.B.'s elemental" (*U*, 152), punning on Blavatsky's postmortem apparition as a vision of her posterior, a true apparition of the afterlife.

Although this Pisgah Sight of the "life esoteric" fuels Stephen's derision of theosophy, he silently examines his own metaphysical beliefs in order to navigate between the rock of theology and the whirlpool of art. Affirming the declaration that he made in "Nestor" upon the nature of God as "noise in the street" to be "very peripatetic," he moves to "space: what you damn well have to see" in an assertion of something that must be there if he, and all things, indeed exist. He continues the meditation on space and visuality by paraphrasing William Blake: "Through spaces smaller than red globules of man's blood they creepy-crawl after Blake's buttocks into eternity of which this vegetable world is but a shadow" (*U*, 153). In Joyce's youthful essay Blake stands as the model of the artist who follows in "formal precision" the "mystical" impulse of Michelangelo's "pure, clean line that evokes and creates the figure on the background of the uncreated void" (*CW*, 221). In the current passage the "uncreated void" is the backdrop of the universe as described in Blake's *Milton*, cited by Gifford: "For every space larger than a red Globule of Man's blood / Is visionary, and is created by the Hammer of Los: / And every Space smaller than a Globule of Man's blood opens / Into Eternity, of which this vegetable world is just a shadow." These lines, also mentioned in Joyce's article on William Blake, locate the creation of space within the body and the construction of art from the "visionary" capacities of the mind. As if to affirm the paradoxical nature of this inversion Stephen paraphrases Augustine's concept of memory and futurity—"hold to the now, the here, through which all future plunges into the past"—in an awareness that, here as in *Portrait*, time in the form of memory must be preserved in order to surmount the void of consciousness and create from nothing.

The discussion of *Hamlet* converges upon the nature of the ghost, whose appearance from insubstantial air perfectly serves Stephen's need to demonstrate creation from the uncreated void, actuality from potentiality. In a miniature example of art from nothing, he defends his "ghoststory" interpretation by asking first, "What is a ghost? . . . One who has faded into impalpability through death, through absence, through change of manners" (*U*, 154). He follows by imagining Shakespeare's creation of the play—"It is this hour of a day in mid June"—and thinks to himself, "local colour. Work in all you know. Make them accomplices," but words fail to overcome the divide between concept and execution. Instead he returns to his priesthood of the eternal imagination, thinking to himself: "Composition of place. Ignatius of Loyola, make haste to help me!" Loyola of course advocated inward visual meditation as a form of prayer, and Stephen's intercession satirically exaggerates its benefit in the making of visual images. His ambivalence toward faith, not only in God but also in his own productivity, shapes his total response to artistry: "I believe, O Lord, help my unbelief. That is, help me to believe or help me to unbelieve? Who helps to believe? *Egomen*. Who to unbelieve? Other chap" (*U*, 176). Stephen requires himself to create art; therefore, he must answer to its origins. If God and Shakespeare, who after God "created most," derive their work from absence and insubstantiality, so too Stephen's art emerges from the "uncreated void" that he believes in and rebels against.

As an artist, then, Stephen himself is his own first creation who holds within himself the manner of all being. He thinks of himself: "Wait. Five months. Molecules all change. I am other I now. . . . But I entelechy, form of forms, am I by memory because under everchanging forms" (*U*, 156). He holds to "the now, the here" in confirmation of actuality but does so through the agency of memory and perception; as he says to Eglington, we "weave and unweave our bodies, . . . from day to day, their molecules shuttled to and fro, so [too] does the artist weave and unweave his image." This passage recalls Pater's *The Renaissance* in its description of subjectivity and impalpability, against whose intellectual context the youthful Joyce asserts poetry's need to strive "against actuality" in order to represent the continuity of being and becoming. In the current passage Stephen reawakens the conversation of his youth described in *Portrait*. He says, "In the intense instant of imagination, when the mind, Shelley says, is a fading coal, that which I was is that which I am and that which in possibility I may come to be" (*U*, 160). The instant of the imagination is, finally, the moment of self-awareness unfixed in time or body. Stephen, like Shakespeare, must therefore write the book of himself in order to assert his place among Eglinton's satiric "seekers on the great quest" who are "mummed in names."

Stephen proceeds toward this self-inscription by confirming the order of reality around him in terms of the nature of divine and human love. In a passage that responds to the question of familial love, Stephen states: "Do you know what you are talking about? Love, yes. Word known to all men" (*U*, 161). He then recalls, somewhat inaccurately, Aquinas' thought upon true love, which desires the good of another against self-interest. The fragmented Latin, "*Amor vero aliquid alicui bonum vult unde et ea quae concupiscimus*" roughly translates, following Gifford, "love wills something to someone will some good when we want a thing desire it." Despite the truncated syntax the overall impression follows the sensibility of the book and of the day. If in *Portrait* Stephen rejects the Church in favor of loving with the "same kind of love," then here he quite literally desires art into being; however, this model of artistic genesis does not escape his self-scrutiny. He tells himself later, after opining on Shakespeare's origin of characterization, "I think you're getting on very nicely. Just mix up a mixture of theolologico-philolological. *Mingo, minxi, mictum, mingere*" (*U*, 168). The origin of Stephen, and of art in general, becomes a mix of theology and philosophy, so that he observes, "Fatherhood, in the sense of conscious begetting, is unknown to man. It is a mystical estate, an apostolic succession, from only begetter to only begotten. On that mystery and not on the madonna which the cunning Italian intellect flung to the mob of Europe the church is founded and founded irremovably because founded, like the word, macro and microcosm, upon the void. Upon incertitude, upon unlikelihood" (*U*, 170). The reality of art, conception, self-construction, and social structure exists from the "uncreated void" of cognitive space. As Stephen continues, "*Amor matris*, subjective and objective genitive, may be the only true thing in life. Paternity may be a legal fiction. Who is the father of any son that any son should love him or he any son" (*U*, 170)? The question of love's origin and direction becomes the ultimate focus of being for Stephen and Bloom, and the final point of the mystical desire for union and illumination.

Stephen describes the nature of that mystical kinship by remarking upon Shakespeare's inclusion of his own name in his plays and recalling his own inscription of language in the features of nature in "Proteus." He notes the process of self-awareness as the moment when one becomes aware of identity and the void from which it springs: "What's in a name? That is what we ask ourselves in childhood when we write the name that we are told is ours. A star, a daystar, a firedrake, rose at his birth. It shone by day in the heavens alone, brighter than Venus at night, and by night it shone over delta in Cassiopeia, the recumbent constellation which is the signature of his initial among the stars" (U, 172). As a boy at Clongowes he situated his name in his notebook relative to the order of the universe. As an adult he inserts himself into the work of art to signify continuity with divine revelation. Confirming this belief in the manifestation of introspective reality as the basis of aesthetics he recycles his thoughts from "Nestor." As a chapter, "Nestor" focuses upon the self-constructing mind of the teacher and artist, seeing the "actuality of the possible as possible" displayed in the weaving of memory and perception. In the present summary of Shakespeare's death Stephen observes that the bard "found in the world without as actual what was in his world within as possible." Shakespeare, the consummate type of the artist, derives work and expression from subjectivity and absence; art, therefore, is the discovery of the search within. In actuality the solipsism of reality prevails: "Every life is many days, day after day. We walk through ourselves, meeting robbers, ghosts, giants, old men, young men, wives, widows, brothers-in-love, but always meeting ourselves. The playwright that wrote the folio of this world and wrote it badly (He gave us light first and the sun two days later) . . . is doubtless all in all in all of us . . . and would be bawd and cuckold too but that in the economy of heaven, foretold by Hamlet, there are no more marriages, glorified man, an androgynous angel, being a wife unto himself" (U, 175). When he leaves the library he affirms these words: "Stephen, greeting, then all amort, followed a lubber jester, a wellkempt head, newbarbered, out of the vaulted cell into a shattering daylight of no thought. What have I learned? Of them? Of me?" Stephen's inquiry arrives at the essence of questioning by placing thought in the recesses of interiority and knowledge of one's self or another under its shadow. The camera obscura of thought produces, by redoublings and contrarieties, the representation of reality within.

Buck Mulligan ends the chapter by satirizing Stephen's philosophy:

"Every Man His Own Wife, or, A Honeymoon in the Hand (a national im-morality in three orgasms)." Buck announces with mock solemnity: "I have conceived of a play for the mummers." Stephen immediately thinks of his own earlier mummery in "Nestor," in which he tutored algebra and situated his sense of identity between guilt over his mother, whose love alone was real, "the only true thing in life," and the intellectual actuality of "Averroes and Moses Maimonides," whose presence was conjured by the numerical symbols that moved in "grave morrice, in the mummery of their letters, wearing quaint caps of squares and cubes" (*U*, 23). In the present section Stephen thinks of "the pillared Moorish hall, shadows entwined. Gone the nine men's morrice with caps of indices" (*U*, 178). The numerical notation of the schoolroom, the "caps of indices," have vanished in this passage, and gone too in the shadowed hall of intellectual mystery is Mulligan's flippancy. Stephen reconfirms the philosophical contour of the chapter wherein, as in "Nestor," he proves by algebra that he himself is his own creator from the "uncreated void" of consciousness. The lassitude of the chapter's close exactly confirms the passive inspiration that guides Stephen. He remembers his dream of the previous evening as a kind of augury: "Last night I flew. Easily flew. Men wandered. Street of harlots after. A creamfruit melon he held to me. In. You will see" (*U*, 179). The shattering daylight of the library foyer dims, and as he escapes his companions his perceptions become revelatory in tone: "kind air defined the coins of houses in Kildare street. No birds. Frail from the housetops two plumes of smoke ascended, pluming, and in a flaw of softness softly were blown." Lyrical and insubstantial, the smoke curls in offering to the idea of contemplation and its equivalency in art. Stephen thinks, "cease to strive," and his ambition, direction, and ordered perception give way to the "peace of the druid priests of Cymbeline: hierophantic: from wide earth an altar" (*U*, 179).

From the "shattering daylight of no thought" in "Scylla and Charybdis" the day's thoughts flow such that "Circe's" assault upon reason comes as the most natural expression of the visual potential of the distorted subconscious mind. In the beginning Stephen waves his ashplant, thereby "shattering light over the world" and in the darkness of the brothel preparing for the discourse of light to come in "Ithaca." By his action Stephen demonstrates to Lynch the real "gift of tongues rendering visible . . . the first entelechy" (*U*, 353). Lynch's reply, "pornosophical philotheology," establishes the core of the chapter—the "metaphysics in Mecklenburgh street," Dublin's brothel district—as the relationship of sexuality and disorder to perception. Haunted by their own sense of the past and fear of the future, his friends make literal Stephen's description in "Scylla and Charybdis" of the life in which "we walk through ourselves, meeting robbers, ghosts, giants, old men, young men, wives, widows, brothers-in-love, but always meeting ourselves" (*U*, 175). In walking through the brothel of the shadow of themselves Stephen and Bloom meet death in ghost form, in hallucinatory meditation designed to question the nature of design. Bloom contorts his face to resemble Moses Maimonides, thus anticipating "Ithaca" in its presentation of personal history and recollection. While Maimonides explores the relation of science to faith, Bloom encounters, rather, his sense of the hidden erotic. Stephen, for his part, invokes the "noise in the street. Self which it itself was ineluctably preconditioned to become. *Ecco!*" (*U*, 412) and enunciates the antagonistic relationship between art and authority, which questions the status of God, Shakespeare, and finally Stephen himself.

In the battle between the pornosophical and the philotheological, the defiled (and deified) body wins over the humanized god. The closing of "Oxen" prepares for the voice of Elijah in "Circe" whose road-show jargon—"Book through to eternity junction . . . Are you a god or a doggone clod?"—urges the listeners to prepare for their second advent with the question "Have we cold feet about the cosmos?" (*U*, 414). The status of both the cosmos and their respective preparedness occupies Stephen and Bloom all day so that the Jerusalem hailed by Elijah becomes echoed by the gramophone as "Whorusalaminyourhighhohhhh." The perspective of the chapter is set; authority, religious or otherwise, emanates from the nether regions of the mind, and art becomes its blasphemous satire and negation. In a chapter in which "Esthetics and cosmetics are for the boudoir" (*U*, 416), the whores whose "high haircombs flashing . . . catch the sun in their mocking mirrors" (*U*, 470) conflate sexuality with religious obscurity. Their mirrors reflect the dark side of Stephen's meditation in "Nestor" in which "Averroes and Moses Maimonides" flash "in their mocking mirrors the obscure soul of the world, a darkness shining in brightness which brightness could not comprehend" (*U*, 23). In this way bodily desire, licit or otherwise, overtakes the imagination. In particular the "obscure soul of the world," so far as the consciousness of "Circe" is concerned, shines forth plainly from the repressed regions of the mind and makes literal the "darkness" of the creative imagination that conjures these visions. Erotic fantasy and desire replace spiritual inquiry as the essence of negative thought.

The origin of fantasy itself, desire, comprises the main theological and psychological point of "Circe." After Bloom declares his delight in sitting where a woman has sat, "especially with divaricated thighs, as though to grant the last favours," the Nymph enunciates a group of associations that identify the relationship of mysticism, absurdity, and art:

THE NYMPH

(eyeless, in a nun's white habit, coif and hugewinged wimple, softly, with remote eyes) Tranquilla convent. Sister Agatha. Mount Carmel. The apparitions of Knock and Lourdes. No more desire. *(she reclines her head, sighing)* Only the ethereal. Where dreamy creamy gull waves o'er the waters dull.

(Bloom half rises. His back trouserbutton snaps.) (U, 450)

The nymph's Carmelite garb recalls at once Bloom's association in "Lestrygonians" of Our Lady of Mount Carmel, the gustatory pleasure of "caramel," and, perhaps, the erotic visual correlative of John of the Cross's diagram of the ascent of the mount at whose center is nothing. The profane context suggests that unlike the sightings of the Virgin Mary at Knock and Lourdes, this nymph in nun's clothing highlights the tension between the world of sexual allure and the relinquishing of desire advocated by the negative mystical tradition. Gifford notes that "Sister Agatha" is Saint Agatha of Sicily, whose martyrdom included residence in a house of prostitution. In the brothel of "Circe" the nymph who declares "no more desire" represents one of the most ascetical Christian orders, whose Doctor Mysticus, John of the Cross, explores the nature of "no more desire" as the quintessential expression of God. The nymph seeks the "ethereal" as the opposite of the substantiality of excitement: "Where the dreamy creamy gull waves o'er the waters dull." However, the irony lies in the fact that all experience in "Circe" lies in the insubstantial territory of the mind. To relinquish desire is to put out the candle of imagination altogether and embark, much as in "Ithaca," on an adventure "through the incertitude of the void."

In "Circe" the nature of that incertitude is death. Stephen envisions his mother's ghost breathing upon him as she says, "All must go through it, Stephen." Stephen, terrified by his own guilt, declares his unwillingness to submit to the universe of human limitation and so invokes "The intellectual imagination! With me all or not at all" as his artistic credo and form of *"non serviam"* (U, 75). Stephen fulfills the action at the beginning of the chapter and with his ashplant shatters the light to the cry of "Nothung." The darkness that naturally ensues is that of nothing, as well as the echo of "Nestor's" vision of history: *"Time's livid final flame leaps and, in the following darkness, ruin of all space, shattered glass and toppling masonry"* (*U*, 475). In "Circe" Stephen has revised the ghost story of "Nestor" to destroy the "form of forms" of his mother and thereby reconstruct his own sense of being through formlessness, impalpability, and fantasy.

The relationship of desire, death, fantasy, and the body culminates in the Black Mass of the chapter's close in its mocking of material revelation. The opening, *"introibo ad altare diabolo,"* echoes the beginning of the book and emphasizes the bloody host, *"corpus meum,"* as its physical theology. The voice of Adonai speaks, "Dooooooooooog!" in recognition perhaps of Stephen's encounter in "Proteus" with the dog in his ritual search upon the beach for the nature of manifestation, a Circean response to his aesthetic *quem queritis*. Bloom tries to remove Stephen from the scene, offering him his stick. Stephen's reply summarizes by its cynicism the point of the chapter: "Stick, no. Reason. This feast of pure reason" (*U*, 490). The feast of the Mass is over; however, their self-devouring doubt perpetually questions the location of truth within the ordinary confines of the senses. As a model of the *creatio ex nihilo*, the chapter repeats Stephen's "Nothung" as the inarticulate and, finally, nihilistic vision of the intellectual imagination, cannibalizing the body of its inspiration to erode ordinary inspiration. In like fashion, Bloom's final ghostly vision of Rudy stares inarticulately at his creator, unable to spring to life.

At the close of this long day Bloom and Stephen in "Ithaca" repair to Eccles Street, where they arrive at sensualized enlightenment intellectually. As part of the chapter's theological structure Bloom must steal into his house, thereby enacting his ritualized and satirized role as bringer of light. After falling over the railings and rising again, Bloom lights a candle. Although a simple and logical act under the circumstances, its emplacement in the darkness of uncertain night flickers with visual and liturgical potential. While probably as old as human awareness, the meditation upon the history of light may be traced first within Greek thought. To Plato the metaphysical value of light lay in its embodiment of the Good, synonymous with being and knowing. This valuation of enlightenment, refracted by Aristotle, shone through the Middle Ages as the *quinta essentia*, the clear light of heaven, and became in the paradoxical rhetoric of the Neoplatonists the point to which all darkness endeavored to return. The writings of Dionysius the Areopagite view light as the vehicle of divine immanence and transcendence whose essence can be known only through a perfect envelopment in darkness. The most pertinent images of light for "Ithaca" appear in liturgical allusions that implicitly draw upon the earlier sources. Used to represent Christ, spoken of in the Nicene Creed as "true light from true light," illumination suffuses the Christmas liturgy and symbolizes the conflation of flesh and spirit, the birth of Christ and the advent of creation. This liturgical cycle ends with the blessing and procession of candles at Candlemas. The feast, which coincides with Joyce's birthday, falls on 2 February and commemorates the meeting in the temple where Christ is proclaimed "a light of revelation to the gentiles." This Christian nativity glimmers in "Ithaca" and elsewhere in the text against the most profound doubt, rendering Bloom, who "had not risked . . . did not expect . . . had not been disappointed," an earnest yet dubious "light to the gentiles" (*U*, 553), whose composure and compassion suggest the value of his ordinary inquiries into knowledge.

Having lit Stephen's entrance from the dark, Bloom prepares a "collation for a gentile" in the form of hot chocolate, and the pair exchange artistic and philosophical visions. Although the chapter suggests that they merge consciousness, their creative ideas indicate a temperamental difference that enables the ever-questioning Bloom to reach a greater spiritual equanimity than the conscience-haunted Stephen. After hearing of Bloom's advertising concept to sell stationery, Stephen offers a moody, evocative scene: "Solitary hotel in mountain pass. Autumn. Twilight. Fire lit. In a dark corner young man seated. Young woman enters. Restless. Solitary. She sits. She goes to window. She stands. She sits. Twilight. She thinks. On solitary hotel paper she writes. She thinks. She writes. She sighs. Wheels and hoofs. She hurries out. He comes from his dark corner. He seizes solitary paper. He holds it toward fire. Twilight. He reads. Solitary" (*U*, 560). Stephen's Romantic mood piece recalls the second act of *Exiles* in which Bertha and Robert tryst. Joyce wrote the play after *Portrait* and before *Ulysses*, drawing on the language of mystical literature to describe the power of sexuality and the nature of uncertainty, deepened by Richard's preference to remain in doubt of his wife's fidelity. In his notes to the play Joyce describes the self-absorbed Richard as an "automystic" (*Exiles*, 113). Richard's final words reveal a psychospiritual quest for the stimulation of desire: "I have wounded my soul for you—a deep wound of doubt which can never be healed. I can never know, never in this world. I do not wish to know or to believe. I do not care. It is not in the darkness of belief that I desire you. But in restless living wounding doubt" (*Exiles*, 112). The wound of doubt that Richard seeks extends beyond the text of *Exiles* and into Stephen's mind, which understands and desires nothing better than its own limitation. In his vision of the hotel meeting he reenacts the central episode of the play—Bertha's encounter with Robert in a remote cottage at night—and subtly reawakens the context of adultery that occasions Bloom's travels. In Stephen's reverie the woman writes "Queen's Hotel" several times, coincidentally the scene of Bloom's father's death, thus prompting Bloom to recount the details of his father's suicide with the chapter's bald precision. Differences of narrative aside, the main distinction between the stories lies in Stephen's attempt at the evocative moment versus Bloom's flat acceptance of painful circumstance. With the same quiescence he brings to Molly's adultery Bloom recounts this other shaping experience that contours his day; Stephen prefers the doubt of night.

Stephen and Bloom's restless doubt and restful certainty order their artistic impulses. As part of their "multiple, ethnically irreducible consummation" in the kitchen Bloom chants in Hebrew the anthem of the Zionist movement; in response to the question "What was Stephen's auditive sensation?" the chapter replies, "He heard in a profound ancient male unfamiliar melody the accumulation of the past," the visual correlation of which is "The traditional figure of hypostasis." Bloom's "visual sensation" is the "young male familiar form" of Stephen who embodies a "predestination of a future"; "auditively" he hears the "traditional accent of the ecstasy of catastrophe" (*U*, 565). Stephen hears the past in Bloom and sees Christ; accordingly, Bloom sees the future in Stephen and hears both stasis and radical change. The chiasmus of their thoughts indicates the relation of sense to perception. For Stephen, Bloom's messianic identity models memory and recognition; hypostasis refers to the union of Christ's divine and human attributes, and Bloom unites homely flesh with the destiny of history, both Christian and Jewish. In this way the mystery of separate identity is solved; Stephen merges Bloom with time and futurity, which already contains the past. Bloom beholds in Stephen a vision of the future which, in the manner of all history, holds within it the rhythm of stasis and death. This synesthesia of time and memory suggests that understanding is relative to sense constructions, and perception tied to a sense of a final moment, either of death or of change. Stephen draws art from his haunted sense of the past; Bloom circularly unites present and future.

That future contains natural conditions such as eating, birth, death, and disasters that "make terror the basis of human mentality," in life's relentless movement "from infancy through maturity to decay" (*U*, 572).

Because of this march to death Bloom leaves to a "superior intelligence" the task of imagining a more acceptable world order. Stephen, assuming the superior role, refuses the "dejection" of Bloom and invokes the "affirmation of the spirit of man" to identify himself as a "conscious rational animal proceeding syllogistically from the known to the unknown . . . a conscious rational reagent between a micro and a macrocosm ineluctably constructed upon the incertitude of the void" (U, 572). Stephen abandons the security of knowledge despite his rationality and accepts the uncertainty that makes the "void" a fine and private place. Bloom, for his part, apprehends this concept "not verbally. Substantially" and moves toward his embrace of the "unknown to the known through the incertitude of the void" (U, 572). Bloom the rational philosopher moves to substantial apprehension through the insubstantial, the void, maybe death; Stephen relinquishes all impulse toward certainty.

Following this dialectic of knowledge and negation both Stephen and Bloom emerge from the house to embark upon the void of darkness. Much as in *The Dark Night of the Soul* in which the lover escapes to meet God in the night, Bloom carrying a candle and Stephen bearing hat and ashplant proceed outward in vaudevillian fashion to encounter the secret of their very being. Their escape by candlelight, alluding at once to Candlemas, the Christmas cycle, and the exodus from Egypt, leads them "*secreto* . . . silently, doubly dark, from obscurity by a passage from the rere of the house" to behold the vastness of the universe with Dantean eroticism: "heaventree of stars hung with humid nightblue fruit" (U, 573). From the immensity of the cosmos to the minutia of bacteria, sperm, and blood, "themselves universes of void space," their envelopment in vast darkness suggests an ever diminishing physical universe in which "nought nowhere was never reached" (U, 574). In exiting the ordered space of the house to the emptiness of the night, Bloom particularly experiences absence. Meditating upon the "pallor" of humans against the vitality of the cosmos, Bloom determines that "it was not a heaventree . . . that it was a Utopia, there being no known method from the known to the unknown" (U, 575), thus affirming (ironically) through negation that his own trajectory from the unknown to the known represents the ideal state of human affairs. Bloom is the antimystic who recognizes fracture and discontinuity in the relationship of the past—historical, racial, personal—with the present. Although he sees the future in Stephen's face, he hears the sound of the past, "which possibly had ceased to exist as a present before its probable spectators had entered actual present existence" (U, 575). Change typifies creation, and the "ecstasy of catastrophe" that defines Bloom's notion of shifts in time and space actually surmounts their limitations so that there is existence prior to actuality. This secular vision of creation, quite literally from nothing, leads to a spiritual union of Stephen and Bloom's opposing temperaments when they urinate simultaneously in the dark; of course, Bloom's artistic vision focuses on the physical problems of "irritability, tumescence, rigidity, reactivity, dimension, sanitariness, pilosity," while Stephen wonders at Jesus' circumcision and whether the "divine prepuce . . . were deserving of simple hyperduly or of the fourth degree of latria" (*U*, 577). Each recapitulates at the level of personality the descent into knowledge through darkness.

Stephen departs for home, having completed his day's journey with a moment of transcendent, detumescent urination. Bloom also returns from exile to add up his day's expenses and contemplate another "orbit" around Dublin, concluding that the "obscurity of the night" and the "uncertainty of thoroughfares" render "departure undesirable." Instead he opts for Mollywarmed bed, "obviating desire and rendering desirable: the statue of Narcissus, sound without echo, desired desire" (*U*, 599). After the day's migration Bloom must reconcile his domestic situation to his philosophical musings. The "sound without echo" reverberates finally from within Bloom, "the statue of Narcissus," whose very being defines the metaphysics of "desired desire," a state of constant anticipation and repose. He catalogues his day in terms of the history of the Jews, with each event corresponding to holy acts and places, concluding with his involuntary apprehension of the "brief sharp unforeseen heard loud lone crack emitted by the insentient material of a strainveined timber table" whose sudden noise evokes the intervention of the spiritual world into human dimension. Gifford notes that Jung recorded just such occurrences as evidence of a real presence, and Bloom's immediate ponderings on the mysterious nature of M'Intosh confirm that the nature of mystery itself defines this night of the soul. In response the chapter asks which enigma Bloom, "having effected natural obscurity by the extinction of artificial light," was able to "silently suddenly comprehend." The answer is the traditional riddle "Where was Moses when the candle went out?" whose response is, naturally, in the dark. Bloom comprehends darkness and its ramifications in his lassitude and equanimity in the face of adultery and the "terror" of the "human mentality." Like the Moses of the riddle who receives enlightenment in obscurity, the Maimonidean side of Bloom strives to preserve guidance in perplexity and acknowledge the possibility of mystery while remaining a literal-minded "conscious reactor against the void of incertitude" (*U*, 604). "Ithaca" ends with Bloom in "silent contemplation," wondering about thought, deciding not to act, finally reducing his thoughts, marriage, and being to *un point bien visible,* the final dot of the chapter, its conclusion as well as its point of origin. For Kabbalah, the original moment of being is the "primordial dot" at the heart of the Zohar, its deepest book. This dot situated between nothing and being signifies the concept of union inherent in the first moment of creation (Scholem, *Major Trends,* 218). This final thought of "Ithaca" serves as the ultimate first word for the verbal creation of "Penelope" and for the larger investigation of the way in which mind and body awaken the imagination to darkness.

Against Bloom and Stephen's visions of futility, death, annihilation, and the "terrors of the human mentality," "Penelope" offers a resolution of body and mind in whose erotic murmur day and night interpenetrate. Molly thinks of her morning card reading, which featured Bloom as "a dark man in some perplexity" (*U*, 640). In her night thoughts she dwells upon Bloom's mixture of scientific and pragmatic traits that incline him toward the philosophic doubt that opposes her sense of the fullness and purpose of life. As the book's conclusion "Penelope" responds to the emptiness of "Circe" and the relentless question of "Ithaca": who searches for meaning and what is the reply? Bloom in his perplexity reenacts the limits of his Maimonidean predecessor despite his more mystical exploration of the body and imagination; Stephen reveals the doubt at the core of his quest for visible meaning. In "Penelope" Molly achieves a secular reconciliation of faith and intellectual constructs by uniting the attributes of God, the imagination, and the origin of creation fully within the terms of the sensual world, working in the lyricism of the chapter's close toward the dissolution of mental and physical division through the power of intense recollection.

Joyce worked hard to eroticize Molly's responses to all aspects of life, including religion and its representatives. In the typescript pages of "Penelope" he inserted in ink notable details that heighten the sexual value of the passages, such as "the palm moist always . . . I wonder did he know me in the box of course he'd never turn or let on" (*U*, 610), in reference Father Corrigan (see Joyce, "Penelope"). But while Molly's sensual freedom needs little documentation, her perception of the spiritual world and its links with the body establishes the union of mind and flesh that inclines toward the affirmation of the book's close. Early in the chapter Molly recalls a stormy night in which she "felt lovely and tired myself and fell asleep as a top" only to waken to thunder: "I thought the heavens were coming down to punish us when I blessed

myself and said a Hail Mary like those awful thunderbolts in Gibraltar
as if the world was coming to an end and then they come and tell you
there is no God" (U, 611). In the typescript pages Joyce inserts a long
passage: "what could you do if it was running and rushing about nothing only make an act of contrition the candle I lit that evening in Whitefriars' street chapel for the month of May see it brought its luck though
he'd scoff if he heard because he never goes to church mass or meeting
he says your soul you have no soul inside, only grey matter because he
doesn't know what it is to have one" (U, 611). Molly tells us in plain
words her belief in a vitality beyond the physical, a soul, which ani-
mates her world and confounds Bloom. The street name is quite deliberate. Joyce originally penned in "William Street," then crossed it out
and wrote "Whitefriars'," an allusion to the Carmelite order. Although
profoundly unascetic, Molly echoes nonetheless the spiritual urges of
Carmelite mysticism—the desire that is fulfilled by the absent presence
of God. Molly answers affirmatively one of the book's most pervasive
questions—is there a presence beyond the material—and endows the
query with positive attributes of creative ability and imaginative potential by drawing from nothing the stuff of her recollection: "as for them
saying theres no God I wouldnt give a snap of my two fingers for all
their learning why dont they go and create something I often asked him
atheists or whatever they call themselves" (U, 643). The God of creative
manifestation appears to Molly imaginatively, sexually and humanly.
Against the *nada* of incertitude Molly unites male and female, past and
present in the model of memory, subjectivity, night, and imagination
upheld in Kabbalah and John of the Cross's poem, as she falls asleep
among the rhododendrons of Howth and the fig trees of the Alameda
gardens. "Proteus'" evocative question "Perhaps there is someone?" is
answered in the erotic and resonant "Yes" of the novel's end, in which
the darkness of the void yields to the presence of the body and the acceptance of the realm of the senses.

5

Night Now!
Waking to Obscurity

Joyce's final work awakens the night of sleep, dreams, and unconsciousness to "mortinatality" (*FW*, 447.8) and its playfully rejuvenescent possibilities. If John of the Cross ends the exegesis of his poem *The Dark Night of the Soul* with the tantalizingly incomplete line "on that glad night," and Molly closes *Ulysses* with an affirmation of eroticism, memory, and sleep, *Finnegans Wake* pursues the "felicitous culpability" (*FW*, 263.29) of the revelation of the aesthetic mind to itself. Among its many subjects, *Finnegans Wake* is about the complexity and merriment of being alive. While *Ulysses* ponders daytime queries into doubt and the "Grandbeyond" (*FW*, 570.1), the *Wake* absorbs itself in the nighttime recollection and anticipation of the various accidents by which most of us came to be and the lively darkness toward which we nightly move. "Life . . . is a wake" (*FW*, 55.5–7), and this night explores how darkness, in its negative mystical determinants, bears upon perception and the senses.

Joyce shapes this darkness according to mystical theology's obscure ontology of the night, retelling the fall from grace that enables art through the union of body and mind. In the *Wake*'s dark night of cognitive renunciation the cloud of forgetting muffles ordinary language and perception in favor of the nondiscursive play of the unconscious, whose pattern of inquiry and discovery resists cultural imperatives of order and reason for a world of obscurity and play. As a secular work the *Wake* purports not to reveal God either within or without but to portray the seeking mind in the work of restful waking, at once thinking and feeling according to the rules of absence and incertitude that lie at the heart of mystical theology's investment in nothingness and insubstantiality, the "allimmanence of that which Itself is Itself Alone" (*FW*,

114

394.33). The "flight of the alone to the alone" originates with Plotinus and inaugurates, for negative mysticism, the tradition of intellectual solitude that nonetheless unites everything in the "pancosmos" (*FW*, 613.12).[1] The manifestation of all things united in their collective and solitary guises fascinates Joyce, and therefore the *Wake* "exteriorises on this ourherenow plane in disunited solod, likeward and gushious bodies with . . . intuitions of reunited selfdom" (*FW*, 394.34–395.1). The text unites body and mind in the concept of a reducible yet transcendent being, perhaps the dreamer and almost certainly the reader, who welcomes the disruption of ordinary perception as the means to insight. This awareness of the self and its kinship with all things resonates with mysticism's introverted quality that values introspection and the emptying of one's own mind as means to knowledge, at once separate and inseparable from the truths of the body. Joyce integrates the medieval mystical tradition into his "treatment of the night"[2] to unite the world of the spirit with that of sense, forming art from the chaotic space of the imagination. This union, in turn, shapes the aesthetic discussions of its final chapter as they inform the metaphysical "Night Lessons" that lie at the core of the book. If in *Ulysses* the voice of Elijah questions the introspection of the day with radical disbelief, then in *Finnegans Wake* the mystical tradition suggests why this night is different from any other night.

In its figuration of negative consciousness the *Wake* probes the *nada* at the center of John of the Cross's mount and his implicit visual and verbal relation between cosmic order and human life. Following its literary predecessor, the *Wake* understands art as the odd conflation of thought and (non)sense that typifies negative cognition: "In the buginning is the woid, in the muddle is the sounddance and thereinofter you're in the unbewised again . . . Silence in thought! Spreach! Wear anartful of outer nocense!" (*FW*, 378.29–33). In the logic of mysticism and the tenor of the *Wake*, the void of nothing expresses the totality of being, thereby defying the limits of expression and sense, bending the expectations of logic and glorifying the "unbewise" state of silence and nonsense. This cosmic sound and silence, signifying nothing, lie at the heart of the *Wake*'s ontology and establish the night of dreams as emblematic of the way in which knowledge becomes nonsense, and sense, created from nothing, finally returns to its primordial state. The inability to know anything with certainty combined with the ability to recognize the connectedness of all experience lies at the heart of the *Wake* and makes the matter (quite literally) of perception into the subject of controversy and representation the topic of hearsay. In this way the book presents understanding itself as the subject of greatest debate, thus describing in "Epistlemadethemology for deep dorfy doubtlings" (*FW*, 374.17–18) not only the letter in the midden of history, ecclesiastical or otherwise, that shapes much of the night's speculation but the epistemological theology of dear dirty Dublin and its unsure, unbewise inhabitants.

This sensualized theology describes a world "erigenating from next to nothing and celescalating the himals and all, hierarchitectitiptitoploftical, with a burning bush abob off its baubletop and with larrons o'toolers clittering up and tombles a'buckets clottering down" (*FW*, 4.36–5.4). In this passage the origins of the universe arise from Erigena, who shaped aesthetics for the Middle Ages by appropriating Dionysius the Areopagite's understanding of light and perception. Erigena absorbed Dionysius' *Celestial Hierarchy*, which determined the medieval intellectual pattern of ranking, in ascent to God, the order of angelic beings. The summit of experience is the encounter with God in the burning bush, and the choice of saints who traverse the ladder—Laurence O'Toole, patron of Dublin, and Thomas à Becket—both generalizes and makes local the ascent and descent from the "himals" that the dreamer envisions. Drunken hod-carrying Tim Finnegan falls off his ladder, landing in the middlesins world of neither angels nor demons and "clitters" up again in all the forms of resurrection offered by the night in a cycle endlessly repeating.

That rejuvenescent imagination converges most powerfully in the visual sensibility of the Middle Ages, enduring through time with such tenacity as "would turn the latten stomach even of a tumass equinous" (*FW*, 93.9), and most artfully developing monastic culture as the representative feature of its religious life. This monastic life, in turn, allows for the "byways of high improvidence that's what makes lifework leaving and the world's a cell for citters to cit in" (*FW*, 12.1). The model of the cell identifies one version of the universe as the monastery, the stage upon which is played the improvident accidental discovery of creativity and interpretation. This fantasy of an original creative moment that makes life worth living connects introspection and inspiration within those cells, with "every monk in his own cashel where every little ligger is his own liogotenente with inclined jambs in full purview to his pronaose and the deretane at his reredoss" (*FW*, 228.26–28). Cashel, of course, is one of the most elaborate and complete of Ireland's monastic remains. The monks in question gaze at their own private parts in solitude, beholding in their "reredoss" not only the visual focal point of the altar but also their mundane seat of enlightenment. The equation of monkish isolation with masturbatory privacy evokes the overall union of prayer and arousal that distinguishes the *Wake's* use of medieval theological material to destroy any notion of the division of mind and body. In this manner the "besieged bedreamt" (*FW*, 75.5) perceives with "deepseeing insight" during prayer on "anxious seat . . . during that three and hellof hours' agony of silence" (*FW*, 75.13–18) that the "thomystically drunk" (*FW*, 510.18) world of the *Wake* reappropriates religion for art and contemplation for the body.

In its accommodation of the mystical culture of the mind to art, HCE's division into Shem and Shaun exemplifies this blend of spiritual and sexual dispositions. In relation to the spiritual universe of the book, Shem is "athemystsprinkled" (*FW*, 153.27), the atheist, antimystical son. In spite of his attitude of unbelief, he casts his irreligiosity in terms of the contemplative tradition. Spying at the keyhole, presumably into his parents' room, he peers with "an eachway hope in his shivering soul, as he prayed to the cloud Incertitude, of finding out for himself . . . whether true conciliation was forging ahead or falling back after the celestious intemperance" (*FW*, 178.31–35). His prayer and obeisance to the "cloud Incertitude" equates the hoped-for glimpse of sexual activity with mental darkness and forgetting as the means to union with God. "Celestious" invokes, once again, Dionysius' *Celestial Hierarchy* and its concept of the movement ever upward to God. This context for reading peeping Shem's action extends into book I chapter vii, in which he is berated for his reprobate ways. His private disposition is examined—"let us pry" (*FW*, 188.8)—and he is found wanting in gratitude and humility: "you have become of twosome twiminds forenenest gods, hidden and discovered . . . anarch, egoarch, hiresiarch, you have reared your disunitied kingdom upon the vacuum of your own most intensely doubtful soul" (*FW*, 188.8–12). Shem's "intensely doubtful soul" situates knowledge of all kinds within the intellectual context of spiritual cognition.

Shaun, contrarily, embodies the saintly disposition that irritates his brother. In the dichotomies of the book he is Thomas à Becket to Shem's Laurence O'Toole, Abel to his Cain, Esau to his Jacob, and numerous other identities and oppositions. He finds himself associated with spiritual knowledge, and he receives information in ways that may only be described as biblical. As part of the book's many burning revelations his voice from the fire echoes as the "voice, the voce of Shaun, vote of the Irish, voise from afar . . . mid the clouds of Tu es Petrus" (*FW*,

407.13–16), and this identity as the rock of the church and pillar of Ireland solidifies Shaun's position as purveyor of higher things. Through clouds and smoke he obscures: "the letter that never begins to go find the latter that ever comes to end, written in smoke and blurred by mist and signed of solitude, sealed at night" (*FW*, 337.11–14). Signed in solitude and sealed at night, the letter of the *Wake's* origins repeats the solitude and darkness integral to the contemplative tradition. Shaun, a smoking "conformed aceticist and aristotaller" (*FW*, 417.16), establishes his relationship to Shem as one who embraces the conflicting response to the material world implied by the roles of ascetic and Aristotelian.

These responses to materiality approach the matter of matter and in so doing suggest one of the central debates of the *Wake*—how to understand perception. After seeing his brother, Shem wonders, "what have eyeforsight" (*FW*, 417.23), thus calling into question the role of sight in particular, and visuality in general, in this night of spiritual cognition. The "spoof of visibility in a freakfog" (*FW*, 48.1–2), which typifies the world of the *Wake*, is summed up quite nicely in the Vulgate quote, roughly translated "eyes they have but they see not, ears they have but they hear not," which is collapsed into a question all about the senses: "*Habes aures et num videbis? Habes oculos ac mannepalpabuat?*" (*FW*, 113.29–30). The dreamer's doubt of God in a sacred context, and of self in a psychological context, establishes the connection between divine and bodily understanding. One of HCE's many epithets, "How culious an epiphany!" (*FW*, 508.11), clarifies the connection, the revelation being the dropping of underpants to reveal "culious" hinds, yet another version of the crime in the park and the monks absorbed in their "reredoss." The Annunciation motifs that proliferate toward the end of the book, the coming of dawn and Easter and other uprisings, solidify the role of epiphanic revelation in the *Wake's* sense of the spiritual basis of perception: "Think of a maiden, Presentacion. Double her, Annupciacion. Take your first thoughts away from her, Immacolacion. Knock and it shall appall unto you! Who shone yet shimmers will be e'er scheining" (*FW*, 528.19–22). The passage puns upon the life and shrines of Mary, ending with her nineteenth century appearance in Ireland at Knock. Its focus is the nature of appearance itself, and the first thoughts that arise from sacred contemplation end in the representation of the saint. Indeed, "scheining" derives from the German word for manifestation. Not only her image, but also the nature of images themselves, originates and endlessly begets in the sacred imagination. The "hallucinian via" (*FW*, 478.13–14), the Eleusinia Via—the Sacred Way—suggests that the implied eschatological purpose of the ancient fertility cults, Eleusinian or otherwise, is fulfilled in the imaginative, sensory consciousness.

The *Wake* expresses this sacred way of perception in a larger sense through the dreamer's repetitive examination of last things—sleep, death, unconsciousness. The reader and dreamer "round up in your own escapology" (*FW*, 428.21–22) both escape the limitations of the daytime world and encounter the finality of death—a death that may, in the logic of the book and religion, come back to life. The Christian study of eschatology finds early exposition in the works of Saint Irenaeus, one of the first great theologians whose thought nicely resonates in the conceptual and artistic order of the night. Irenaeus developed the idea of recapitulation as part of his theory about the nature of Christ. In this theory previous forms of God from past ages are summed up in the incarnation, which in turn holds all phases of human development; in other words, in Christ "here comes everybody," and fallen humanity is restored to God. That the "inception and the descent and the endswell of man is *temporarily* wrapped in obscenity" (*FW*, 150.30–32) makes sense; time moves according to the mystical and sexual vagaries of the mind as part of the process of enlightenment.

Joyce knew Irenaeus' role in the development of Christian eschatology and employed the idea of recapitulation to suggest not only the pattern of redemption but also the making of images, "for ancients link with presents as the human chain extends, have done, do and will again as John, Polycarp and Irenews eye-to-eye ayewitnessed" (*FW*, 254.8–10). John the Apostle, Polycarp, and Irenaeus are historically linked. Irenaeus knew Polycarp as a young man, and wrote that Polycarp "had intercourse with John and with the rest of those who had seen the Lord" (*ODCC*, 1107). Joyce borrows from Irenaeus the symbols of the four evangelists, which find their way into medieval art and the modern *Tunc* page of the Book of Kells. Although Saint Jerome established the current use of the symbols, identifying Mark with the lion and John with the eagle, Joyce identifies the origin of the images within the historical construction of his Christian material: "The prouts who will invent a writing their ultimately is the poeta, still more learned, who discovered the raiding there originally. That's the point of eschatology our book of kills reaches for now in soandso many counterpoint words" (*FW*, 482.31–34). In the beginning was poetic inspiration, and its expression, verbally and visually, forms the goal of the *Wake*, the "book of kills" whose gospel preaches the fundamental unity of body and mind, origin and destiny, in art.

Joyce's sense of the shared origin and destiny of Ireland and Spain contributes to his enthusiasm for John of the Cross's art and literature. In *Ulysses* Molly is born in Spain, and her recollections of Gibraltar fuse with the memory of Howth in the final moments of the novel. Joyce liked the historical association of "Iar-Spain" (*FW*, 50.20), which unites the Irish word for west with the idea of the west coast of Ireland, which still bears a Spanish influence. Speaking as Saint Patrick, the next link in Joyce's association of John-Polycarp-Irenaeus, Shem inquires of his brother the nature of his creative thought. Observing that the "triptych vision passes" and "deliciated by the picaresqueness of your irmages," he asks if his "iberborealic imagination" has ever considered the possibility of someone else dying for him, a "complementary character, voices apart" (*FW*, 486.34–487.4). The idea of a substitution in death resembles the sacrifice of Christ, and the picaresque view offered by the combined Spanish and northern "iberborealic" imagination suggests that the theology of grace offered to a fallen world results in the playful imaginative consciousness of the artist, John of the Cross or otherwise, whose concept of the crucifixion and subsequent ascent of the mount offers a "deliciated" image to the world.

The delectation of the night finds its intellectual, aesthetic, and erotic center in Joyce's conflation of the "barefaced carmelite" (John of the Cross) with "Padre Don Bruno" (*FW*, 50.19–21), thus invoking not only his biographer but also, of course, Giordano Bruno.[3] John, the "postoral lector" (*FW*, 374.17), took as part of his spiritual mission the tutelage of novitiates as well as the composition of his *Obras*, as his works are called, and in the *Wake* it is Shaun, whose name derives from John, who embodies his identity: "that soun of a gunnong, with his sabaothsopolettes, smooking his scandleloose at botthends of him! . . . I grandthinked after his obras . . . and for to salubrate himself with an ultradungs heavenly mass" (*FW*, 343.23–29). The smoke of mystical inspiration hangs about the *Wake*'s indulgent and licentious version of the writer of the *Obras Espirituales*, and his obscene mass leads Shaun to conclude, "of manifest 'tis obedience and the. Flute!" (*FW*, 343.36) in recognition of the book's repeated assertion that the manifestation of the mind follows upon the urge to know. The glory of this fall into sin and the making of *Obras* expresses the Wakean understanding of the power of John of the Cross's images of dark learning. John's poem and its exegesis become tropological models for Joyce's inebriate images of the night, and the following section will suggest some correspondences between the *Wake* and *The Dark Night of the Soul* before applying this schema to readings of longer passages. "So, to john for a john, johnajeams, led it be!" (*FW*, 399.36).

En una noche oscura / One dark night,[4]

Finnegans Wake occurs in the sleeping dark of HCE's mind, which reaches into the consciousness of all people, past and present. While his changing name suggests multiple identities and behaviors, its elusiveness resonates with the apophatic impossibility of naming God. He represents the "map of the souls' groupography" (*FW*, 476.33); as family man and bearer of sexual guilt his nocturnal omissions consistently elide the truth, whatever it may be, of his "crime" in Phoenix Park. This "foenix culprit" (*FW*, 23.16) obsessively affirms, through denial, the happy fact of his fall, which establishes sexual transgression as the fundamental act of knowledge and ultimate source of unknowing, incertitude, and mystery. This "holinight sleep" (*FW*, 192.19) corresponds with the night of sensory and spiritual purgation advocated by John of the Cross and described in *The Dark Night of the Soul* because the dreamer contemplates the nature of understanding through introspection. In a self-reflexive passage Joyce refers to his semiblind composition of the *Wake* as the antithesis of the clarity of *Ulysses*, "his usylessly unreadable Blue Book of Eccles, *édition de ténèbres*," composed with "aisling vision" (*FW*, 179.26–31). *Finnegans Wake* is the evening edition of the book of experience, which limits ordinary vision and encourages the perception of nothing in particular. It is the "tenebrous *Tunc* page of the Book of Kells" (*FW*, 122.22–23), which reinscribes the importance of unknowing for the intellectual structure of the mystic and artistic night. In the drifts of sleep the "tale told of Shaun or Shem" comes at "night now!" and the river, Anna Livia Plurabella, meets the dreamer in the "hitherandthithering waters of. Night!" (*FW*, 215.35–216.5).

The literal sleep of the *Wake* begets the darkness that, in the paradox of mystical discourse, permits spiritual wakefulness. The alert slumber of the dreamer mimics the language and logic of contemplation, describing a "clearobscure" (*FW*, 247.34) world that values obscurity, clouded vision, and uncertainty unto themselves and as mental states that allow the "secret" night sins of the "underworld of nighties and naughties" to which one must "close your, notmust look!" (*FW*, 147.29). The contemplative metaphor of shutting one's eyes to the world in order to see God reflects the central question of knowledge for the *Wake*: how to perceive with certainty through the vagaries of rumor, history, and memory. In keeping with the parlance of the mystical tradition upon which this aspect of the night is based, the dreamer abandons the world of sense and reason and, relinquishing all sensibility, comes to the essence of negative perception: "It darkles . . . all this our funnanimal world . . . We are circumveiloped by obscuritads" (*FW*, 244.13–15). The mounting dark hides the world of phenomena and animal pleasure in the muffled veilings of obscurity, here presented with a Spanish flair. Yet the veil is also that which covers the holy of holies in Exodus and is torn at the moment of Christ's death, his release from the "funanimal" world, and serves in "Proteus" to pose questions of the infinity of the imagination. Thus the afterlife of the dreamer presents life beyond the limitations of the flesh. The disposition of HCE inaugurates the spiritual topography of the night; "this man is mountain and unto changeth doth one ascend" (*FW*, 32.5) and the ascent of the mount figures in HCE's shifting and dissolving identity in the climb ever inward into John of the Cross's "mount of knowledge" (*FW*, 245.15). He at once desires nothing and everything, repressing the simplest facts of his life while fully participating in all of history and being. In so doing he reinstates the investment in sensual, sensory perception that is fundamental to the negative mystical tradition exemplified by the *Dark Night*. The sleeper's intellectual resemblance to the posture of contemplation grants extraordinary insight into the impossibility of certainty and the certainty of nothingness; "Ichts nichts on nichts!" (343.20) combines the idea of negativity—no—with the echo of night, or *nacht*, and creates an appropriate pun for the shifting of blame in the incident in the park as well as for the condition of seeking knowledge in nothingness, dark, and night.

con ansias, en amores inflamada, / fired with love's urgent longings
oh dichosa ventura / —ah, the sheer grace!—

John of the Cross's speaker embraces literal and conceptual darkness and becomes spiritually aroused toward God. In *Finnegans Wake* the dreamer loses all sense of logic and discursive reason in the night, finding in flesh and sensuality—the fall, the crime in the park, assorted indiscretions—the nature of desire and the urge toward knowledge. When the "darkpark's acoo with sucking loves" (*FW*, 245.17–18), the things that go bump in the night become manifest. Desires and anxieties come to the fore, and the intellect makes representative dreams from their grist, "for its never dawn in the dark but the deed come to life . . . upon the night of the things of the night" (*FW*, 328.27–32). The central imaginative moment for Christianity occurs in the fall, responsible for the creative consciousness that desires knowledge, and figures in the *Wake* as the quest for the sacred in the profane. The "jaculation from the garden of the soul" (*FW*, 145.25–26) becomes the ultimate expression of the location of the postlapserian imagination at play, reinventing itself in terms of its theological origins and reaching toward the act of self-expression that begets art.

sali sin ser notada / I went out unseen,
estando ya mi casa sosegada / my house being now all stilled.

John of the Cross begins his exploration of the night of the spirit by disciplining the senses and quieting the mind in order to leave behind memory, will, and identity and know nothing. In the *Wake* the dreamer likewise loses all sense of time and space, and thus disoriented perceives his sleeping wife, sons, and daughter according to their nocturnal roles in his reenactment of the day. The house from which HCE's mind roams is the pub, family life, and the edifice of civilization. Although he sleeps, his mind wakes and makes him the "mysterbuilder" who, in darkness, leaves the house of the body and the mind only to encounter it in manifold ways. Having "closed the portals of the habitations of thy children," the dreamer puts to sleep the world of ordinary perception so that "thy children may read in the book of the opening of the mind to light and err not in the darkness which is the afterthought of thy nomatter" (*FW*, 258.31–33). In the parlance of negative mystical theology, "nomatter" yields the greatest enlightenment; in the world of the *Wake*, the nothing of sleep provides the means by which one can move unseen, because unseeing, from the daytime world to the more vivid presentation of thought and feeling beyond its limitations.

A oscuras y segura, / In darkness, and secure,
por la secreta escala disfrazada, / by the secret ladder, disguised.

The spiritual ladder originates in Jacob's dream and informs the mystical tradition as a symbol of the ascent of the soul that aspires to God. The ladder stands as a metaphor for the construction of steps, necessary to the human mind, for spiritual progress; nonetheless it remains rooted on earth and implies the possibility of return to a more worldly state. In *Finnegans Wake* the dreamer escapes from the house of the day by "slittering up" and "slettering down" (*FW*, 114.17–18) language, thought, and the book in cloaked identity. Tim Finnegan, who falls off his ladder to seeming death, only to resurrect at his own wake, provides the most immediate example of the descent into chaos and hilarity afforded by unsuccessfully "celescalating the himals." For HCE "with his ladder up" (*FW*, 390.5), the world is revealed in darkness when "in his excitement the laddo had broken exthro Castilian" (*FW*, 91.36–92.1). The excitement of the night, dark and Spanish, breaks from usual artistic genesis and speaks ex cathedra to the variations on truth and the value of uncertainty in their telling. Humpty Dumpty's tumble offers one of the most repeated versions of slittering down the ladder and suggests one way in which HCE becomes himself: "Hung Chung Egglyfella now speak he tell numptywumpty . . . Secret things other persons place there covered not. How you fell from story to story" (*FW*, 374.34–36). By a ladder, in secret, HCE falls from story to story through the time marked by memory and the space noted by his bodily dimensions. In so doing he reenacts the spiritual history of Christianity as a form of enlightened revelry, "thomystically drunk . . . lairking o'tootlers with tombours a'beggars" (*FW*, 510.18–19), falling down drunk into mystical insight.

oh dichosa ventura / —ah, the sheer grace!—

Twice in the poem John of the Cross invokes the concept of grace to explain the divine means by which the soul moves from the night of the sense to that of the spirit, and again from the night of the spirit toward the darkness of mystical union. In the logic of the *Wake* HCE and all others are saved by the intervention not of God but of the essentially compassionate and good-humored nature of people themselves, who repeat their existences in the dreamer's being and thereby in "the pigs of cheesus" although it is "about a pint of porter" (*FW*, 511.19). The picture of Jesus, the image of Christ in whom Joyce saw all people, inspires the intellectual structure of the *Wake*; however, it is the holy waters of the tavern that replenish the draught of the spirit with their "plinary indulgence" (*FW*, 319.7–8). In its explanation of "manifest tis obedience" (*FW*, 343.36) the dreamer responds to the theology of grace as a "pelagiarist" (*FW*, 525.7), invoking the Pelagian concept of the freedom to choose good of one's own accord (*ODCC*, 1058). The *Wake* suggests a world of human motive and disposition that plagiarizes from "story to story" the overall pattern of redemption that stands outside of time because it is circumscribed by the cyclical nature of history and private life. The "pelagiarism" that typifies the art of the *Wake* is a mental gift resulting from the abandon of reason and, in Joyce's youthful words on Dionysius in his article on William Blake, from the "falling

into ecstasy . . . before the divine obscurity, that unutterable immensity"
(*CW*, 222) that permits art.

a oscuras y en celada, / in darkness and concealment,
estando ya mi casa sosegada / my house being now all stilled.

To John of the Cross the spiritual value of darkness, concealment, and
stilled thought lies in its potential to bring about the intellectual emptying that leads to God. In *Finnegans Wake* the cognitive abandon of the
night presents darkness and secrecy as the alternative to ordinary perception. The escape from the senses leads, in the logic of all dark nights,
to an investment in sensuality all the greater for its resistance to the
body. The *Wake*'s method of "courting daylight in saving darkness"
(*FW*, 321.18–19) suggests that the courting of bodies and minds brings
about a kind of reconciliation of the daytime world with the more real,
to Joyce, reality of the mind in the body. In the tradition of the *Cloud of
Unknowing* from which John of the Cross borrows, mystical understanding metaphorically occurs under a cloud of forgetting. In *Finnegans Wake* it occurs "*inter nubila numbum*" (*FW*, 506.31), which McHugh
construes as "among clouds a splendor," invoking not only the revelation of the clouds that cloak Mount Sinai at Moses' ascent, but also the
presence of Issy in her cloudy recirculation back to ALP. The splendor
among the clouds unites the moment of inspiration with the more rib-
ald "numbum" whose splendor teasingly reveals all and nothing. The
sexual revelation parallels the aesthetic and intellectual project in its
fullest form, which is "vurry nothing . . . It amounts to nada in pounds
or pence . . . for the whole dumb plodding thing" (*FW*, 521.3–9). The
work of the artist, like the contemplation of the mystic, leads to the
perception of the relative, discrete nature of experience and the necessity of moving, from story to story, through the construction of truth.

En la noche dichosa / On that glad night,

John of the Cross stops the explication of *The Dark Night* at the entrance to the night. His abandonment of the work with the suppression
of the senses and the loss of faculties described in the previous stanza
suggests that the work is incomplete because it reflects the absence
sought in contemplation. *Finnegans Wake* presents the concept of structural absence that leads to enlightenment through the circularity of its
design. From the final release of the senses in the death of the river to
its recirculation back again into the beginning of the book the stories
conclude in a fusion of past and present that suggests that the "escapal-

ogy" of the night lies in the escape from the house of ordinary being into a different system of time. All has already happened and its status as truth gives way and the value of uncertainty becomes the Joycean equivalent of falling into happy darkness: "I see now. We move in the beast circuls . . . Hillcloud encompass us!" (*FW*, 480.24–26). The physical act of sight reveals the "funanimal" circles of beastly phenomena that shape our perception while at the same moment figuring in HCE the envelopment in cloudy unknowing that typifies the night. The "Real Absence" (*FW*, 536.5–6) appropriates eucharistic theology to the purpose of showing that Christ's presence in the sacrament has a literal as well as symbolical correlation with the presence of all, by the circularity of recapitulation, within the body of the dreamer, which nonetheless strives for the nothingness of the river meeting the sea in the night of the *Wake*.

Book II chapter ii takes as its exposition the biography of John of the Cross as well as an unholy parody of *The Dark Night*. The chapter is written, "honest to John" (*FW*, 448.32), in order to demonstrate that "as no es nada" (*FW*, 470.1) the untranscendent picture of "jam of the cross" (*FW*, 448.8) makes felicitous play of the workings of the spiritual consciousness and the images that it produces. The ascent of the mount becomes the descent into the literalized sexuality of the night in "the greenest island off the black coats of Spaign" (*FW*, 447.27–28). In this vision of "Iereny allover irelands" (*FW*, 455.8) the spiritual night of John of the Cross is recapitulated in the body of the dreamer in the escapades of Shaun. The cover of dark prompts Shaun/Jaun to "take leave of his scolastica" (*FW*, 431.23) and tutor his sister Issy in the ways of carnal love, much as San Juan instructs novices in the path of the divine. Rising to orate, Jaun expresses in the "night we will remember" his "hard suite of affections" for his novice sister (*FW*, 432.2). He says Mass, delivers a homily, and generally dispenses immoral advice for her instruction. His "love's urgent longings" shape his imagination, and, "phonoscopically incuriosited" (*FW*, 449.1) he looks to her for visual pleasure: "before my upperotic rogister, something nice" (*FW*, 439.26).

Issy wants "to get outside monasticism" (*FW*, 456.17) but stands no chance against the "White Friars out on a rogation stag party" (*FW*, 447.18–19). She is the "mainsay of our erigenal house" (*FW*, 431.35) to whom the brothers Shem and Shaun look for erotic as well as imaginative stimulation. The "house" San Juan leaves is that of the senses and intellect for the nada of understanding. Jaun departs his "scolastica" as well to "go forth, frank and hoppy . . . from our nostorey house, upon this benedictine errand but it is historically the most glorious mission, secret or profound" (*FW*, 452.15–18). Shaun's play resonates with the same search for understanding that motivates John of the Cross's poem, and the egress from the house in the happy renunciation of certainty and clarity precipitates the descent into the obscurity of dark and secrecy whose nature the *Wake* seeks to define. Jaun falls irrevocably into sexual sin that bears as its mark the desire to conceal, in darkness, its evidence. He writes "onanymous letters" (*FW*, 435.31) whose mystified authorship recollects the ambiguity of the night of the spirit, subsuming ideas and affect under the "epistlemadethemology" of mystical practice.

The murkiness of Jaun's instructions for the devout gives way to the delights of the night: "when yon clouds are dissipated . . . we shall be hooked and happy . . . among the fieldnights eliceam, *élite* of the elect, in the land of lost time" (*FW*, 453.30–33). This vision of the glad night toward which the dark of renunciation will lead prophesies not only physical pleasure but also spiritual delight in the willing descent from consciousness. The chapter, much like the poem, ends with the promise of revelation in which "the sombrer opacities of the gloom are sphanished!" (*FW*, 473.20) and the dark night of John of the Cross illumines with the promise of mystical union the tenebrous pages of the *Wake*.

In book IV of the *Wake*, Joyce traces contemplation through a conscious examination of the "triptych" stained glass window that structures the chapter to demonstrate how noncontemplative minds nonetheless see the world through a glass brightly. In an often cited letter to Frank Budgen, Joyce states: "In Part IV there is in fact a triptych—though the central window is scarcely illuminated. Namely the supposed windows of the village church gradually lit up by the dawn, the windows, i.e., representing on one side the meeting of St. Patrick (Japanese) & the (Chinese) Archdruid Bulkely (this by the way is all about colour) & the legend of the progressive isolation of St. Kevin, the third being St. Laurence O'Toole, patron saint of Dublin; buried in Eu in Normandy" (Ellmann, *Letters* 1:406).[5] The triptych roughly corresponds to the division of set pieces within the chapter—the description of Saint Kevin, the debate between Berkeley and Saint Patrick, and the flowing out of Annalivia into the sea. Read together these sections provide a model for mystical introspection, understanding, and its reconciliation with light, sight, and the visible world. The triptych structure invokes altarpieces generally and their visual depiction of the narrative of heaven which turns the mind upward and inward. In Joyce's description the elements of the window correspond to the discussions of perception and the practice of mysticism that abound in the text and that, taken as a whole, suggest that the process of aesthetic representation begins in the restfully awake mind of the artistic consciousness. The presence of Laurence O'Toole relates the esoteric and philosophical implications of the first two panels by suggesting Dublin, civic life, and the service of the sacred to the temporal order implied by both the life of the saint and the flowing out of the River Liffey from the Wicklow mountains in which he lived.

The flowing out of *Finnegans Wake* moves to dawn, Easter, and other risings from the night in which things come to pass and come to "Be! Verb umprincipiant through the trancitive spaces" (*FW,* 594.2–3). Dawn originates from the dark, the gospel, physics, the medley of dreams, and the silence of nothing. This last chapter backlights the night of the book by suggesting that revelation, muffled in darkness and obscurity, gets expressed much like the light of illumination of the Dionysian tradition. The metaphor of dawning knowledge and insight literally awakens the dreamer to the prospect of understanding, "a flasch and, rasch, it shall come to pasch" (*FW,* 594.16–17), blending the Hopkins-like epiphanic moment with the pascal fire of rejuvenation and coming Easter. This first glimmer of light infuses the sleeper with the consciousness of waking up and rouses the body to life through the quickening of the heart and blood. These "streamsbecoming" not only of the river but also of the enlivened senses evaluate the night's sleep—"You mean to see we have been hadding a sound night's sleep?"—and tally the night's pleasures in the spiritual terms of the "bathouse and the bazaar, allahallahallah," before concluding that it was "a sot of a swigswag, systomy dystomy, which everabody you ever anywhere at all doze. Why? Such me" (*FW,* 597.1–22). In his essay upon William Blake, Joyce characterized the work of Swedenborg and all mystics as presenting the infusion of spirit in sense captured by "the systole and diastole of love" that expressed creativity. In this passage the dawn of the body is also that of the universe and thought, and the next passage looks to the penetrating light typical of images of the annunciation: "Lok! A shaft of shivery in the act, anilancinant . . . Where did thots come from . . . a flash from a future of maybe mahamayability through the windr of a wondr in a wildr is a weltr as a wirbl of a warbl is a world . . . It is perfect degrees excelsius" (*FW,* 597.24–31). The light through the window captures the past in the present moment, investing in the body of the dreamer the recapitulation of spiritual history. Temperature and blood pressure rise, and as the "torporture" returns to "mornal" the moment of stirring consciousness fuses with the making of art: "Humid nature is feeling itself freely at ease with all the fresco" (*FW*, 597.31–34). In this moment of "Be," time and space lose relevance so that "then's now with now's then in tense continuant" (*FW*, 598.28–29), implying a moment of understanding that clarifies relationships by looking beyond discursive order. This final chapter both concludes and begins the inquiry into the things of the night by initiating the mystical quest suggested in its opening: "A hand from the cloud emerges, holding a chart expanded" (*FW*, 593.19). The map descends from the clouds and implies that the ascent of the mount begins here, guiding the reader through the labyrinth of the dark.

Dawning consciousness, perception, and visual representation arise quite literally from the dark night of the soul. From the clouds emerges a synopsis of the book that also circles back to its origins: "Nuctumbulumbumus wanderwards the Nil. Victoria neantas. Alberths neanthas. It was a long, very long, a dark, very dark, an allburt unend, scarce endurable, and we could add most quite various and somenwhat stumbletumbling night. Endee he sendee. Diu!" (*FW*, 598.5–9). The clouds of night wander toward the Nile, the nil, and the nought. The Victoria and Albert reservoirs of the river equally hold nothing and imply likewise the absence of meaningful cultural, political, and social order. The drawn-out description of the night echoes the first line of *The Dark Night* poem—"On a dark night"—suggesting that the night river flowing to the sea merges as fully with nothingness as do the lives contained therein; however, this nothingness that arises from the night's efforts toward unconsciousness evokes the mystical approach to the attainment of knowledge. While in *Portrait* Stephen recants his heresy of the soul's approach to God, in *Finnegans Wake* it is precisely this "coming nearer" that Joyce seeks to express. The "supernocturnal" (*FW*, 598.17) efforts of the night coalesce in the dreaming body of HCE, "Cumulonubulocirrhonimbant heaven electing," whose cloudy reorientation permits the spiritual eroticism inherent in the release of self-consciousness and descent into mystery: "the dart of desire has gored the heart of secret waters and the poplarest wood in the entire district is being grown at present, eminently adapted for the requirements of pacnincstricken humanity" (*FW*, 599.25–28). The penetration of the secret, sacred heart by desire appropriates the language of mystical ecstasy to suggest enthusiasm as a form of resistance against the existential panic of nothingness. The ability to mistake the forest for the trees and construe absence for abandonment, as opposed to enlightenment, typifies the struggles of the night; it is, in effect, a lapse of faith. Yet these lapses constitute the business of living, "all the goings up and the whole of the comings down and the fog of the cloud in which we toil and the cloud of the fog under which we labour" (*FW*, 599.29–31), ceaselessly repeating the pattern of spiritual ascent and descent through unknowing that characterizes the night of the soul. In the chapter of the coming of the dawn the quest for certainty pours, like the "Nil," into the "Polycarp pool" (*FW*, 600.5) of eschatological history from which it springs.

The first of the triptych panels dips into the polycarp pool of Saint Kevin. Toes first, the narrative eases into a Latinate description "Of Kevin, of increate God the servant," who, seeing the forest in the trees, goes to "the tall timber" in "the search for the love of knowledge through the comprehension of the unity in altruism through stupefaction" (*FW*, 604.27–33). Kevin, the model of the ascetic Irish saint, sought the isolation of his monastery in Glendalough, which is located in the Wicklow mountains from whose source the Liffey flows. Kevin retreated for extended periods, and when asked to become bishop agreed with great reluctance and only out of the conviction that God called him from the comfort of renunciation as a spiritual duty. Nonetheless, he sought the loneliest hilltop in the area and built a beehive hut for his retreat. In the *Wake* he transforms into the "procreated" priest whose "*altare cum balneo*" soaks him in knowledge of all varieties. McHugh points out that Kevin's description repeats at some point all of the cardinal virtues, the ranks of angels, the sacraments, and the canonical hours. He further suggests, obscurely, that the variations provided upon the word *create* suggest the presence of *Celestial Hierarchy* and *Ecclesiastical Hierarchy*. These are the names of two of the four works of Dionysius the Areopagite, which set forth the order of angelic beings and all things within the universe. Kevin achieves his exalted awakening at "matin chime" in his mountain retreat, "amiddle of meeting waters of river Yssia and Essia," derivatives of the modern Irish words for he and she. The meeting of the waters in Kevin's tub and altar unites the sexual impulses of the night in the "lawding" of the "triune trishagion" that supplants prayer with intercourse. The bawdy lauding converges upon the "supreem epicentric lake Ysle . . . whereon by prime, powerful in knowledge, Kevin came to where its centre is among the circumfluent watercourses" (*FW*, 605.16–19). Dionysius used the image of the center of the sphere whose circumference is unknown as a depiction of God's ineffability. In the spiritual topography of the night the nature of centering itself, of locating the seat of being and thought, defies normal processes and finds expression only in the sexual knowledge of the body. Cardinal points in hand, so to speak, Kevin gauges his location according to the orientation of the "honeybeehivehut in whose enclosure to live in fortitude" (FW, 605.24), retreating to the lake isle of inner spaces in monastic solitude. More or less situated, he takes up the reform of followers and "exorcised his holy sister water, perpetually chaste," both chasing and chastening her to fill his tub. Thus enthroned he "sat in his sate of wisdom, that handbathtub," receiving his holy insight, like the monks of Cashel, from the handy seat of inspiration as "*doctor insularis* of the universal church, keeper of the door of meditation, memory *extempore* and proposing and intellect formally considering" (FW, 606.7–9). For Kevin as for all mystics, meditation, memory, and intellect inform the contemplative exercise, here yielding in its watery nascence the "primal sacrament of baptism or the regeneration of all man by affusion of water. Yee" (FW, 606.9–10). Contemplation merges with its origins, uniting each new generation in understanding.

If in the triptych vision of Kevin contemplative habits of mind and body exemplify thought, then the Saint Patrick and Archdruid Berkeley correlative panel demonstrates how this thought translates into art. The episode of Mutt and Jute precedes this section and offers a model of Kevin's thought. Muta poses the question "quodestnunc fumusiste volhvuns ex Domoyno," which McHugh translates to mean "what now is that smoke rolling out of the Lord?" Juva's reply confirms the smoky identity of the Lord as the "Old Head of Kettle puffing off the top of the mornin" (FW, 609.24–25). Smoke and revelation conspire to show that "Dies is Dorminus master," suggesting that the celestial order supersedes the obscurity of night to reveal, potentially, the "wolk in progress," which conflates the Dutch word for cloud with Joyce's original title for *Finnegans Wake, Work in Progress.* The cloud of unknowing that metaphorically shrouds the thought in progress descends again upon the two, and their ensuing conversation attempts to determine how knowledge is processed in terms of the book. Their chat turns to the model of Berkeleyan philosophy, which asserts that reality inheres in the mind against the empirical assumptions of ordinary perception: "Bulkily: and he is fundementially theosophagusted over the whorse proceedings" (FW, 610.1). This declaration supports Berkeley's philosophy over the weak-mindedness of theosophy, yet jokingly implies that his ineffable worldview, much like that of Kevin and the Cashel monks, has a "fundementially" solid base. The "whorse proceedings" that follow recount the tale of Buckley and the Russian general, and by implication all battles that inspire confusion and debate. This debate resolves in the impossibility of resolution, concluding only that unity leads to diversity, which leads to combat and again to appeasement, agreed upon in the already suspect "light of bright reason."

This light becomes the subject of the following debate upon "rhythm and colour" (*FW*, 610.34) between Berkeley and Patrick. In this conversation Archdruid Berkeley asserts the unknowability of reality against the pragmatism of Patrick's belief in the ease of representation. The debate presents another version of conflict—at once political, familial, and theological—in which, this time, the optics of light suggest that aesthetic perception itself relies upon an understanding of the mind as open to possibilities. Beginning with the "Tunc" of the Book of Kells page encountered in other discussions of aesthetics, the vision of the Archdruid reveals a perspective that accommodates the abundant color in the universe. The apprehension of color, like beauty, emerges from the smoky "photoprismic velamina of hueful panepiphanal world spectacurum of Lord Joss" (*FW*, 611.13–14). In this filmy, obscure version of reality, the act itself of perceiving color draws the viewer into his own mind, creating the perceived object, so that "he savvy inside true inwardness of reality, the Ding hvad in idself id est" (*FW*, 611.21). Like the inward gaze of Kevin and the Cashel monks, the Archdruid's introspection permits the understanding of the body that the more rationalistic Patrick resists. The "thing which it unto itself is," which motivates perception, is the id of desire, whose drives contemplative practice seeks to engage and subsume. Instead of knowing the true inwardness of reality, which echoes the mystical preoccupation with interiority, Patrick begins his speech with the conclusive "Punc," which limits the aesthetic discussion by inserting the finality of a period into his statements. The "petty padre" categorically denies multiplicity and subjectivity by viewing the world "shiroskuro," quite literally in black and white terms. As a form of insult he suggests that the Archdruid is "aposterioprismically apatstrophied and paralogically periparolysed" (*FW*, 612.18), shining multicolored reality from his posterior and therefore unable to reason correctly. Patrick asserts the validity of his logic by demonstrating the truth of the trinity through the form of the shamrock, thereby using his "sound sense sympol" to elicit assent. In their debate Patrick appears to have the upper hand by speaking last; however, the book's investment in asserting the primacy of the senses and the fluidity of representation makes Patrick a theological buffoon, alien to the mystical tradition that aligns philosophically with the sensual subjectivity of Archdruid Berkeley.

The *Wake* "idself" concludes not with Patrick's authoritarianism but with the theological openness that implies that mystical thought allows for the intuitive knowledge of the body and thereby constructs reality. In reiteration of the physical and mystical origin of the night that moves to dawn, Joyce's systole and diastole of love and wisdom "receives through a portal vein the dialytically separated elements of precedent decomposition," which recombine "by the ancient legacy of the past, type by tope, letter from litter" into the homey scramble of breakfast and renewed life that begins the day (*FW*, 614.36–615.1). This recapitulation of the night's courses implies that enlightenment of all sorts takes place through the body of the sleeper—"yon clouds will soon disappear looking forwards at a fine day" (*FW*, 615.17)—yet the denouement of the tale belongs to Annalivia. Her egress to the darkness of the sea and death suggests the sensual caress of her waters against the outlining form of her husband "and me as with you in thadark" (*FW*, 622.15), but her final parting sadly laments facing death "ourselves, oursouls alone. At the site of salvocean" (*FW*, 623.28–30). Joyce said he planned another book after *Finnegans Wake*, to take up the subject of the ocean. In its absence the end of the *Wake* points to the void in which all nights originate and to which they flow, poetically recounting the spiritual excursion that brings us ever round to "scale the summit!" (*FW*, 624.11).

The "chart expanded" of book IV maps the recirculation back to darkest night at the center of the book, the "Night Lessons" pursued by the children. In this chapter, the final and most dense of its composition, the children learn their "triv and quad" at the knee of monastic culture and show, through their ambivalent relationship to cognition, the mystic's model of knowing truth through accepting the nada of darkness. This model of nothingness, based on the dark night of John of the Cross, follows the ascent of the mount of learning and forgetting in order to arrive at the sensual realities of the body that express the subjective nature of tuition and intuition through the relative certainty of sexuality. As a model of mystical illumination the chapter, like John of the Cross's diagram of the ascent of Mount Carmel, displays an imaginative consciousness that nothing, in fact, is all. As a model for the intellectual and aesthetic premises of the *Wake*, the final chapter explains why "ours is mistery of pain" (*FW*, 270.22) that nonetheless resolves into pleasure.

The central chapter of *Finnegans Wake* is sometimes labeled chapter X, and it is a critical commonplace to read the symbol for ten as a cross, marking the intersections of lives, histories, and interests. When read in the context of John of the Cross's mystical tradition, the imposition of the figure upon the chapter of darkest night suggests the union of his image of ascent with Joyce's own diagram of the attainment of knowledge at the chapter's end. The tutoring by night demonstrates that intellectual cognition, suppressed in the mystical night, imparts enlightenment only when discursive thought gives way to the faculties of the body. The chapter begins in the Berkeleyan milieu that calls ordinary perception into question and establishes subjective philosophy as the handmaid of aesthetics. The narrative similarly resists traditional order by relegating the observations of the boys to marginalia and the witticisms of Issy to footnotes, thereby establishing the rebellion against order, whose overthrow permits the incursion into metaphysical darkness. In the pubhouse the children study upstairs, the patrons drink downstairs, and the order of the house mimics that of the universe, "since primal made alter in garden of Idem. The tasks above are as the flasks below . . . in a more and more almightily expanding universe" (*FW*, 263.20–26), which allows for the alternative knowledge of "felicitous culpability." This night school meets to find out the "maymeaminning of maimoomeining" (*FW*, 267.3). The meaning of meaning inheres in the search for the moment "where flash becomes word and silents selfloud" (*FW*, 267.16–17), the utterly interior union of revelation, understanding, and union toward which the "flasch" of dawn in book IV moves. The knowledge sought by the children resides entirely within the moment of introspection, wherein the riddle of being resolves into the relative perspective of the inquisitor: "The allriddle of it? That that is allruddy with us, ahead of schedule, which already is plan accomplished from and syne" (*FW*, 274. 2–5). The quote holds forth the comfort of already being in destiny, without the limitations of time or space and within the fold of history. In essence, the model of recapitulation that informs the body of the dreamer sustains the commonality of the night in the moment of insight. This intuitive "flash" emerges from the mystical tradition of intellectual renunciation: "After sound, light and heat, memory, will and understanding" (*FW*, 266.18–19). The senses kindle the body, and the recitation of the medieval ascent to cognition recalls the willing subversion of precisely those functions necessary for mystical enlightenment. Following their intellectual forebears, the children too resist memory, will, and understanding in order to grasp the relevance of their lesson by night.

The concept of memory underpins the premise of learning—one studies, presumably, in order to retain ideas, make associations, and thereby order the world. The text presents an assault upon this model of study by violating the associations of knowledge with certainty, thus upsetting traditional ideas of authority and power. In their effort to reconcile ideas to the intimate lessons of the unconscious, the children scribble, doodle, and thereby express the primacy of the associative intellect that refuses rote memorization in favor of anagogic relationships. In creating their own "idem" of play, they relate to the outside world by speculating upon their own origins as only inwardly focused creatures can. Shaun, echoing the theological tenor of their instruction, observes that they review "GNOSIS OF PRECREATE DETERMINATION. AGNOSIS OF POSTCREATE DETERMINISM" (*FW*, 262) in their exploration of creation and creativity, physical and artistic, as it relates to the process of knowing. Unlike Shaun's pedantry and Shem's insouciance, Issy's footnotes reflect startling cynicism at the finality and inevitability of sexual knowledge: "One must sell it to some one, the sacred name of love" (*FW*, 268, footnote 1). Against the memory of the primal scene sought by the boys, Issy foregrounds the more immediate memory of sexual relations and thus affirms, darkly, the primacy of bodily recollection as a form of surety. This concept of memory held in the body repeats the structure of the contemplative tradition, which relinquishes the overt memories of the body yet relies upon their stimulation. While the children study, the tutorial voice that guides them parenthetically reflects upon the pattern of learning: "*leo* I read, such a spanish, *escribibis*, all your mycoscoups" (*FW*, 300.16–17). The three r's are rolled on the Spanish tongue of an intellectual mentor who regards the reading and writing of the children as the crux of the "mythemathematics" that they both resist and remember.

The "iberborealic" imagination of HCE, "Hispano-Cathayan-Euxine, Castillian-Emeratic-Hebridian, Espanol-Cymric-Helleniky" (*FW*, 263.12–15), determines the children's universe and pitches the memorization of algebra, geometry, and other ancient sciences against the assertion and suppression of will. In questioning the identity of the God of Kabbalah, "Ainsoph . . . Who is he? Whose is he? Why is he? Howmuch is he? Which is he? When is he? Where is he? How is he?" (*FW*, 261.23–31), the chapter dissolves the issue of fixity into one of volitional perception. Kabbalah, like its mystical counterparts in Christianity, acknowledges the infinitude and indefinability of God. Any representation, any answer to the questions posed above becomes tantamount to an act of will that falsely resists ambiguity and satisfies only the most relative, imprecise questions about God or anything else. Instead, the loosening of will required of the contemplative grants to the physical body the perception of knowledge beyond that of discursive reason. The literal night so befogs sight that "you must proach near mear for at is dark" (FW, 297.14–15), visibly illuminating the contours of the subject while invisibly extending the limits of perception beyond the eye into the suppression of will in the mystical night of understanding. The visual outlines of self and other merge in a sort of identity game: "you must have the proper sort of accident to meet that kind of a being with a difference" (FW, 269.14–15) in which physical being, in the absence of will, permits the desire for the knowledge of God; answering the question "Who is he?" both represses and releases the visual libido of the night. The accident of being forms a body, the apprehension of which repeats that of aesthetic perception—"beauty life is body love" (FW, 271.9)—folding art into the body and perception into the mystery of knowing.

The aesthetics of mystical representation necessitate forgetting the world of ordinary perception and turning the will, as in "Ithaca," toward "desiring desire." The contemplative tradition from which these concepts arise admits the possibility of divine union, or understanding, from their practice. In the heart of night understanding is relative, arbitrary, and leads to the expression of the "nada" at the core of experience. The children's search for original meaning pursues the possibilities of divine union to discover the "diminitive that chafes our ends" (FW, 278, footnote 2). Their search for the bottom line brings them to the diagram of their mother's vagina, from which they originate and to which their thoughts, directly or indirectly, return (see figure 3). The "mythemathematics" lesson of the night presents the children struggling with their algebra. McHugh identifies "Coss" as the "rule of Coss," which derives from the Arabic word for unknown quantity. The search for the unknown through the known, Bloom's mission in "Ithaca" and the children's quest in the textbook, reaches a point of insight in the geometric representation of the body. Losing oneself in "some somione sciupiones" (FW, 7–8) dreamworld suggests the renunciation of faculties that begins the moment of mystical apprehension. The figure of the mother equally represents the beginning of apprehension both in and out of the womb, as Shaun's note indicates: "Uteralterance or the Interplay of Bones in the Womb." Sensibility emerges through the birth canal, which "heaving alljawbreakical expressions . . . of specious aristmystic unsaid" is simply the origin of thought, expression, and art. The center of the diagram, and therefore of the children's inquiry, recalls the summit of experience at the head of John of the Cross's ascent. The saint's sketch and Joyce's drawing represent the cognitive abandon that leads to negative enlightenment, in both instances through the sensual physiology of the body.

In searching for the unknown the children study the diagram, trying to discern whether it is

greater THaN or less THaN the unitate we have in one or hence shall the vectorious readyeyes of evertwo cicumflicksrent searclhers never film in the elipsities of their gyribouts those fickers which are returnally reprodictive of themselves. Which is unpassible. Quarrelary. The logos of somewome to that base anything . . . comes to nullum in the endth. (*FW*, 298.13–22)

They compute that union leads to reproduction, which, like a film loop, repeats backward and forward the whole of being. Concluding that one cannot reproduce oneself they decide that their origins lie in nothing. The side note wryly indicates that this pattern of apprehension is based in spiritual matters by echoing yet again Dionysius the Areopagite's works of negative theology: "*Ecclesiastical and Celestial Hierarchies. The Ascending. The Descending.*" The children partially solve for the unknown by searching for it in its own negative terms. Again on the same page Shaun reiterates that their inquiry follows the "*peripatetic periphery*" whose marginalia points the way to truth. The text that this note glosses describes the nothing of the "paradismic perimutter, in all directions on the bend of the unbridalled, the infinisissimalls of her facets becoming manier and manier as the calicolum of her umdescribables (one has thoughts of that eternal Rome)" (*FW*, 298.29–34). All roads lead to the summit of John of the Cross, the vortex of Annalivia in which "*Omnius Kollidimus*" (*FW*, 299.8), and circle back again to the Dionysian center of the sphere.

The figuring of their mother's figure reveals to the children not only their biological but also their intellectual origins in darkness and unknowing. The leap of Cartesian faith that teaches them to "cog it out, here goes a sum" (*FW*, 304.31) proves false in the dark periphery of consciousness. Their peripatetic wisdom points instead to the tradition of mystical thought for the solution to the mystery of unknowability. Shem's excesses of the night, "LIPPUDENIES OF THE UNGUMPTIOUS" (*FW*, 308), reassert the value of the visual libido of the unconscious mind, which permits Shaun's "*Consummation. Interpenetrativeness. Predicament. Balance of the factual by the theoric Boox and Coox, Allmallagamated*" (*FW*, 308). The theory of the "*Boox and Coox*" fuses John of the Cross's ascent of the night with the penetration of mystery inherent in the quest for the unknown. The ascent to nada seeks unconsciousness of the flesh but finds enlightenment within its terms, begetting in its turn the moment of apprehension and the representation of art. Annalivia's encroaching dawn and dying light present this moment of artistic inspiration between death and regeneration, epiphany and apocalypse, "as on the night of the Apophanypes" (FW, 626.4–5), in which "something fails us. First we feel. Then we fall" (FW, 627.11). The failure is the glorious one into humanity and art that creates, in Joyce's words on William Blake, the "pure, clean line" drawn in darkness from the sensual imagination and inscribed upon the void of space.

In *Finnegans Wake* Joyce draws that line in darkness by creating a work that reflects the "sensual philosophy" of mystical aesthetics. John of the Cross's eroticized theology turns absence to understanding and nothingness to art. In so doing he puts to sleep, among the lilies of his poem, ordinary consciousness and perception in favor of forgetting and the approach to nada. His diagram of the ascent of the mount figures the release of desire as desire itself, and the subsequent descent into nothingness as the summit of subjectivity. In their approach to ineffability and the epistemology of unknowing, both the writings of the mystics and the *Wake* explore the revelation of the mind to itself. It is this revelation that had artistic consequences for Joyce's contemporaries, as well as for his own work. Read from this perspective, the *Wake* focuses upon the mind of the dreamer as the most actual and real of subjects.

In its attention to the most real absence, *Finnegans Wake* explores the making of the subject itself by illuminating the development of the artistic imagination. In *Ulysses* Joyce employs concepts from the mystical tradition in order to present artistic consciousness as the reconciliation of the self to the unknown, in which the movement toward absence nonetheless occurs through the body and material reality. The *Wake* culminates Joyce's investigation into the artistic implications of mystical thought by embracing the body as the center of knowledge and its recesses as the loci of understanding. In so doing he replaces reason with the mystery of erotic and philosophic uncertainty, and through humor approaches the deepest profundity of thought. As Saint Kevin bathes he begins his contemplative exercises in "the search for love of knowledge." His meditation is fulfilled in the night lessons of the children, which lead to the revelations of the dawn, in which the real mysteries of being, "the miracles, death and life are these" (FW, 605.2–3). Be sure to laugh.

Notes
Bibliography
Index

Notes

Chapter 1. Medieval Abstrusiosities: The Negative Mystical Tradition

1. All quotations from *The Cloud of Unknowing* are taken from the Early English Text Society edition, but I have transliterated the medieval characters.

2. All quotations from the poem are taken from the translation offered by Kieran Kavanaugh and Otilio Rodriguez in *The Collected Works of St. John of the Cross*.

3. All references to the prose work *The Dark Night of the Soul* are taken from Peers.

4. Peers (193) notes that the saint lived for many years after abandoning the manuscript. That he died, and therefore left the work incomplete, is suggested only by the Alba de Tormes MS.

Chapter 2. Against Actuality: *Critical Writings* in Context

1. While there is substantial evidence of Joyce's familiarity with Pater, there is no documentation of his knowledge of Thompson, Thomson, or Hopkins. The purpose of this chapter is to argue not for Joyce's certain acquaintance with their writing but rather for his immersion in the literary and intellectual habits of mind exemplified by their work.

2. The phrase "the revelation of the mind to itself" is taken from the essay "Winklemann" in *The Renaissance* (184).

3. The link between Pater and Joyce is pursued in only a few sources, the most pertinent to the study of aesthetics being Poirier's. Poirier attributes scholarly negligence of Pater's seminal influence upon modernism, and particularly Joyce, to ignorance of Pater's complexities and deliberate obfuscations that suggest the tension between "ascesis" in style and ineffability in subject. Poirier argues that to understand Pater in this manner provides "an alternative criticism" that points to the radical subjectivity at the heart of Pater's writing, modernism's development, and Stephen Dedalus' character. Scotto remarks on the primacy of sight as an analogy to self-knowledge in their works. Perlis focuses upon Pater's "unfettered" sensation as the aesthetic quality that fosters the amorality of Joyce's fiction. See also McGowan for an assessment of Pater and Joyce's relationship to modernist concepts of being and dissolution.

Chapter 3. The Esthetic Image: The *Portrait* of Sensation

1. Yates (46) observes the relation between Augustine's philosophy and the medieval concept of memory as it contributes to the image-making power of the mind.

2. Beja follows Joyce's definition of the term "epiphany" to signify a "sudden spiritual manifestation, whether from some object, scene, event, or memorable phase of the mind" (18). He understands the term "epiphany" to mean the manifestation of Christ and finds it significant as a moment of revelation, although he refrains, rightly, from equating such a moment with mystical experience, whose hallmarks he lists as denial, annihilation of the self, intuitive insight, nonlogical reasoning and mortified senses. Instead, he adheres to a secular interpretation of Joyce's use of the term, suggesting that it is a figure of speech rather than a signifier of true religious emotion. For this reason he dislikes Hugh Kenner's suggestion in *Dublin's Joyce* that "it is radically impossible to understand what Joyce is talking about from the standpoint of the post-Kantian conviction that the mind imposes intelligibility on things . . . It is things which achieve epiphany under the artist's alchemical power, and not his own soul which he manifests . . ." (Kenner, 138). In his rejection of Kenner's position, Beja implies that Joyce simply rejects the content of his religious rearing while preserving its form for artistic purposes. Citing the example of Augustine, he suggests that the early medieval ideas of the psychological existence of time and the primacy of memory in the intellect change, by the Romantics, into a "secular epiphany" that preserves the usual distinctions of mind and body, subject and object. More recently Gifford succinctly points out that overreliance on that definition can lead to confusion. The manifestation of the object reveals its "whatness," its individuality, and the practical application of this idea to the stories in *Dubliners* leaves in doubt which of the many possibilities implicit in the stories constitutes its epiphanal revelation. Instead, Gifford thinks the term applies to the "precise handling of detail along with the author's refusal to point, evaluate, or interpret in any direct way the meaning of a detail" (Gifford, 3).

3. In spite of Wolfhard Steppe's recent article, which reads "epicleti" as an error for "epiclets," I am inclined to agree with the interpretive scholarship that argues for the term's logic within Joyce's writing.

4. In her formative article Florence Walzl aligns the transformative property of the epicleti with the creative process of the artist, and identifies the epiphany as the result or manifestation of his work.

5. The actual quotation as translated by Henry Chadwick is "Grant me chastity and continence, but not yet" (Augustine, 145).

Chapter 4. Getting on Nicely in the Dark: Perception in *Ulysses*

1. Among other literary efforts Clifford Bax also edited *The Golden Hind* and *The Hero and the Man*, by A.E.

2. See chap. 3, p. 65.

Chapter 5. Night Now!: Waking to Obscurity

1. See chap. 1, p. 14.

2. Joyce identifies John of the Cross's text as one of the two most central for the "treatment of the night" in the composition of his final work; see chap. 1, p. 8, for further discussion.

3. Cumpiano suggests that Joyce may have read the standard biography of the saint, written by Father Bruno. She traces the influence of Saint John's life as a plot-structuring device for the *Wake*, assigning to the twins the role of acting out both his charismatic preaching and his torturous imprisonment.

4. The translation is taken from *Collected Works*, 50–51.

5. This quotation first appears in full in Glasheen's *First Census*. As she remarks in a footnote in the *Third Census* on the letter from which the quote is taken which does not appear in *Letters*, "I don't know who gave it to me. If the letter was not forged by Jim the Penman (q.v.), or dug up by a hen (q.v.), I guess its date to be just before Joyce's letter to Budgen, 20 August 1939 (*Letters*, I, 406)" (Glasheen, lxviii).

Bibliography

Atherton, James S. *The Books at the Wake: A Study of Literary Allusions in James Joyce's Finnegans Wake.* Carbondale: Southern Illinois UP, 1959, 1974.

Aubert, Jacques. *The Aesthetics of James Joyce.* Baltimore: Johns Hopkins UP, 1992.

Augustine, Saint. *Confessions.* Trans. Henry Chadwick. New York: Oxford UP, 1991.

Averroes. *Tahafut al-Tahafut (Incoherence of the Incoherence).* Trans. Simon Van den Bergh. London: Luzac, 1954.

Bayer, Hans. "The Phoenix in the Desert: Neoplatonic Mysticism as Reflected in Twelfth/Thirteenth Century Literature and Criticism." *Studia Mystica* 11, no. 4 (Winter 1988): 32–59.

Beja, Morris. *Epiphany in the Modern Novel.* London: Peter Owen, 1971.

Benedictine of Stansbrook Abbey. *Mediaeval Mystical Tradition and St. John of the Cross.* London: Burns and Oates, 1954.

Benson, A. C. *Pater.* English Men of Letters. New York: Macmillan, 1906.

Berkeley, George. *The Works of George Berkeley.* Vol. 1. Eds. A. A. Luce and T. E. Jessop. London: Thomas Nelson and Sons, 1948.

Biale, David. *Eros and the Jews: From Biblical Israel to Contemporary America.* New York: Basic Books, 1992.

Bishop, John. *Joyce's Book of the Dark: Finnegans Wake.* Madison: U of Wisconsin P, 1986.

Bloom, Harold, ed. *Selected Writings of Walter Pater.* New York: Columbia UP, 1974.

Boardman, Brigid M. *Between Heaven and Charing Cross: The Life of Francis Thompson.* New Haven: Yale UP, 1988.

Boehme, Jacob. *The Signature of All Things, With other Writings.* New York: Everyman's Library, 1912.

Bonaventure, Saint. *Itinerarium Mentis in Deum.* Trans. Philotheus Boehner. Saint Bonaventure, N.Y.: Saint Bonaventure University, 1956.

Bottala, Paola, Giulo Marra, and Franco Marucci, eds. *Gerard Manley Hopkins: Tradition and Innovation.* Ravenna: Longo Editore, 1991.

Boyle, Robert. *James Joyce's Pauline Vision.* Carbondale: Southern Illinois UP, 1978.

Brivic, Sheldon. *Joyce the Creator.* Madison: U of Wisconsin P, 1985.

Brooks, Peter. *Christian Spirituality: Essays in Honour of Gordon Rupp.* London: SCM Press, 1975.

Buckler, William E. *The Victorian Imagination. Essays in Aesthetic Exploration.* New York: NYU Press, 1980.

Buckler, William E. *Walter Pater: The Critic as Artist of Ideas.* New York: NYU Press, 1987.

Bundy, Murray Wright. *The Theory of the Imagination in Classical and Medieval Thought.* Illinois Studies in Language and Literature, 12, nos. 2, 3 (1927).

Byron, Kenneth Hugh. *The Pessimism of James Thomson in Relation to his Times.* London: Mouton, 1965.

Campbell, Joseph, and Henry Morton Robinson. *A Skeleton Key to Finnegans Wake.* New York: Penguin, 1972.

Child, Ruth C. *The Aesthetic of Walter Pater.* New York: Macmillan, 1940.

Christ, Carol. *The Finer Optic: The Aesthetics of Particularity in Victorian Poetry.* New Haven: Yale UP, 1975.

Cloud of Unknowing, The. Ed. Phyllis Hodgson. EETS, 218. London: Oxford UP, 1944.

Colledge, Eric. *The Medieval Mystics of England.* New York: Charles Scribner's Sons, 1961.

Cumpiano, Marion. *Saint John of the Cross and the Dark Night of Finnegans Wake.* Colchester: A Wake Newslitter Press, 1983.

Day, Robert Adams. "Dante, Ibsen, Joyce, Epiphanies, and the Art of Memory." *James Joyce Quarterly* 25, no. 3 (1988): 357–62.

De Laura, David. *Hebrew and Hellene in Victorian England: Newman, Arnold, and Pater.* Austin: U of Texas P, 1969.

Dictionary of the Middle Ages. Ed. Joseph R. Strayer. 13 vols. New York: Charles Scribner's Sons, 1982.

Dictionnaire de spiritualité ascétique et mystique. Ed. Marcel Viller. Paris: G. Beauchense et ses fils, 1937.

Dobell, Bertram. *The Laureate of Pessimism: A Sketch of the Life and Character of James Thomson ("B.V.").* London: Published by the Author, 1910.

Dobell, Bertram, ed. *The Poetical Works of James Thomson.* Vol. 1. London: Reeves and Turner, 1895.

Eco, Umberto. *The Aesthetics of Chaosmos: The Middle Ages of James Joyce.* Cambridge: Harvard UP, 1989.

Elder, E. Roseann, ed. *The Roots of the Modern Christian Tradition.* Kalamazoo: Cistercian Publications, 1984.

Ellis, Virginia Ridley. *Gerard Manley Hopkins and the Language of Mystery.* Columbia: U of Missouri P, 1991.

Ellmann, Richard. *James Joyce.* Oxford: Oxford UP, 1982.

Ellmann, Richard, ed. *The Letters of James Joyce.* Vols. 2 and 3. New York: Viking, 1966.

Ellmann, Richard, ed. *Selected Letters of James Joyce.* New York: Viking, 1975.

Encyclopedia Judaica. Ed. Cecil Roth and Geoffrey Wigoder. Jerusalem: Keter Publishing House.

Encyclopedia of Philosophy. Ed. Paul Edwards. 4 vols. New York: Macmillan, 1967.

Encyclopedia of Religion. Ed. Mircea Eliade. 15 vols. New York: Macmillan, 1987.

Fellows, Jay. *Tombs, Despoiled and Haunted: "Undertextures" and "After Thoughts" in Walter Pater.* Stanford: Stanford UP, 1991.

Fletcher, Ian. *Walter Pater.* London: Longmans, 1959, 1971.

Gifford, Don. *Ulysses Annotated: Notes for James Joyce's Ulysses.* Berkeley: U of California P, 1988.

Giles, Richard F., ed. *Hopkins among the Poets: Studies in Modern Responses to Gerard Manley Hopkins.* International Hopkins Association Monograph Series #3. Hamilton, Ontario, 1985.

Gillespie, Michael Patrick. *James Joyce's Trieste Library: A Catalogue of Material at the Harry Ransom Humanities Research Center.* Austin: U of Texas P, 1986.

Glasheen, Adeline. *Third Census of Finnegans Wake.* Berkeley: U of California P, 1977.

Glasscoe, Marion. *English Medieval Mystics: Games of Faith.* London and New York: Longman, 1993.

Glasscoe, Marion, ed. *The Medieval Mystics of England.* Dartington Hall: D. S. Brewer, 1987.

Glasse, Cyril. *The Concise Encyclopedia of Islam.* San Franciso: Harper and Row, 1989.

Gordon, John. *Finnegans Wake: A Plot Summary.* Syracuse: Syracuse UP, 1986.

Gose, Elliot B. *The Transformation Process in Joyce's Ulysses.* U of Toronto P, 1982.

Harper, Ralph. "The Return Journey: Some Theses on the Ontological Imagination." *Modern Language Notes* 97 (1982): 1121–28.

d'Hangest, Germaine. *Walter Pater: L'homme et l'oeuvre.* Paris: Didier, 1961.

Healy, George H., ed. *The Complete Dublin Diary of Stanislaus Joyce.* Ithaca: Cornell UP, 1962.

Herring, Phillip F. *Joyce's Uncertainty Principle.* Princeton: Princeton UP, 1987.

Hough, Graham. *The Last Romantics.* London: Gerald Duckworth, 1949.

Inge, William Ralph. *Studies of English Mystics.* Freeport, NY: Books for Libraries Press, 1969.

Inman, Billie Andrew. *Walter Pater's Reading: A Bibliography of His Library Borrowings and Literary References, 1858–1873.* New York: Garland, 1981.

James, William. *The Varieties of Religious Experience.* New York: Collier, 1961.

John of the Cross, Saint. *The Collected Works of Saint John of the Cross.* Trans. Kieran Kavanaugh and Otilio Rodriguez. Washington, D.C.: Institute of Carmelite Studies, 1991.

John of the Cross, Saint. *Selected Writings.* Ed. Kieran Kavanaugh. New York: Paulist Press, 1987.

Johnson, William. *The Mysticism of "The Cloud of Unknowing."* Wheathampstead: Anthony Clarke, 1987.

Joyce, James. *The Critical Writings.* Ed. Ellsworth Mason and Richard Ellmann. Ithaca: Cornell UP, 1989.

Joyce, James. *Exiles.* New York: Viking, 1951.

Joyce, James. *Finnegans Wake.* New York: Penguin, 1980.

Joyce, James. *A Portrait of the Artist as a Young Man.* New York: Viking, 1964.

Joyce, James. *Stephen Hero*. New York: New Directions, 1944.

Joyce, James. *Ulysses*. New York: Random House, 1984.

Joyce, James. *Ulysses:* [a portion of] "Penelope." typescript, 26 pp., 1921. HM 41122. Huntington Library, San Marino, CA.

Keller, Joseph. "The Function of Paradox in Mystical Discourse." *Studia Mystica* 6, no. 3 (Fall 1983): 3–19.

Kenner, Hugh. *Dublin's Joyce*. New York: Columbia UP, 1987.

Knowles, David. *The English Mystical Tradition*. New York: Harper, 1961.

Knowles, David. *The Nature of Mysticism*. London: Burns and Oates, 1967.

Lagorio, Valerie Marie, and Ritamary Bradley. *The Fourteenth-Century English Mystics: A Comprehensive Annotated Bibliography*. New York and London: Garland, 1981.

LeBuffe, Francis. *The Hound of Heaven: An Interpretation*. New York: Macmillan, 1921.

Lichtmann, Maria. *The Contemplative Poetry of Gerard Manley Hopkins*. Princeton: Princeton UP, 1989.

Louth, Andrew. *The Origins of the Christian Mystical Tradition from Plato to Denys*. Oxford: Clarendon Press, 1981.

Mackenzie, Norman H., ed. *The Poetical Works of Gerard Manley Hopkins*. Oxford: Clarendon Press, 1990.

Magill, Frank N., and Ian P. McGreal, eds. *Christian Sprituality*. San Francisco: Harper and Row, 1988.

Maimonides, Moses. *The Guide for the Perplexed*. Trans. M. Friedlander. New York: Dover, 1956.

Mandrell, James. "Rending the 'Veils' of Interpretation: San Juan de la Cruz and the Poetics of Mystic Desire." *Revista Canadiense de Estudios Hispanicos* 15, no. 1 (Autumn 1990): 19–32.

McCarthy, Patrick. "The Structures and Meanings of *Finnegans Wake*." In *A Companion to Joyce Studies,* eds. Zack Bowen and James F. Carens. Westport: Greenwood Press (1984): 559–633.

McGinn, Bernard. *The Foundations of Mysticism*. New York: Crossroads, 1991.

McGinn, Bernard, John Meyendorf, and Jean Leclerq, eds. *Christian Spirituality: Origins to the Twelfth Century*. Vol. 16 of *World Spirituality: An Encyclopedic History of the Religious Quest*. New York: Crossroads, 1989.

McGowan, John. "From Pater to Wilde to Joyce: Modernist Epiphany and the Soulful Self." *Texas Studies in Language and Literature* 32, no. 3 (1990): 417–45.

McGrath, F. C. *The Sensible Spirit: Walter Pater and the Modern Paradigm*. Tampa: U of South Florida P, 1986.

McHugh, Roland. *Annotations to Finnegans Wake*. Rev. ed. Baltimore: Johns Hopkins UP, 1991.

Megroz, R. L. *Francis Thompson: The Poet of Earth in Heaven. A Study in Poetic Mysticism and the Evolution of Love-Poetry*. New York: Charles Scribner's Sons, 1927.

Meynell, Everard. *The Life of Francis Thompson*. London: Burns and Oates, 1913.

Milosh, Joseph E. *The Scale of Perfection and the English Mystical Tradition.* Madison: U of Wisconsin P, 1966.

Morse, J. Mitchell. *The Sympathetic Alien: James Joyce and Catholicism.* New York: NYU Press, 1959.

Nadel, Ira B. *Joyce and the Jews: Culture and Texts.* Iowa City: U of Iowa P, 1989.

New Catholic Encyclopedia. Ed. William J. McDonald. New York: McGraw-Hill, 1967.

Noon, William T. *Joyce and Aquinas.* New Haven: Yale UP, 1963.

Norris, Margot. *The Decentered Universe of Finnegans Wake.* Baltimore: Johns Hopkins UP, 1976.

North, John S., and Michael D. Moore. *Vital Candle: Victorian and Modern Bearings in Gerard Manley Hopkins.* Waterloo: U of Waterloo P, 1984.

O'Conor, J. F. X. *A Study of Francis Thompson's Hound of Heaven.* New York: John Lane, 1912.

Oxford Dictionary of the Christian Church. Ed. F. L. Cross. London: Oxford UP, 1974.

Pater, Walter. *Appreciations with an Essay on Style.* New York: Macmillan, 1901.

Pater, Walter. *Marius the Epicurean: His Sensations and Ideas.* Oxford: Oxford UP, 1986.

Pater, Walter. *The Renaissance: Studies in Art and Poetry.* Ed. Donald L. Hill. Berkeley: U of California P, 1980.

Peers, E. Allison. *Studies of the Spanish Mystics.* Vol. 1. London: Sheldon Press, 1927.

Perlis, Alan D. "Beyond Epiphany: Pater's Aesthetic Hero in the Works of Joyce." *James Joyce Quarterly* 17, no. 3 (Spring 1990): 272–78.

Pick, John. *Gerard Manley Hopkins: Priest and Poet.* London: Oxford UP, 1942.

Poirier, Richard. "Pater, Joyce, Eliot." *James Joyce Quarterly* 26, no. 1 (Fall 1988): 21–35.

Pope, Myrtle Pihlman. *A Critical Bibliography of Works by and about Francis Thompson.* New York: New York Public Library, 1959.

Prioleau, Elizabeth. "The Nights of Gerard Manley Hopkins: A Mystical Starscape." *Victorian Poetry* 21, no. 1 (Spring 1983): 85–91.

Pseudo-Dionysius. *Complete Works.* Trans. Colm Luibheid. New York: Paulist Press, 1987.

Rabate, Jean-Michel. *Joyce upon the Void: The Genesis of Doubt.* New York: St. Martin's Press, 1991.

Raitt, Jill, ed. *Christian Spirituality: High Middle Ages and Reformation.* Vol. 17 of *World Spirituality: An Encyclopedic History of the Religious Quest.* New York: Crossroad, 1988.

Reynolds, Mary T. *Joyce and Dante: The Shaping Imagination.* Princeton: Princeton UP, 1981.

Riehle, Wolfgang. *The Middle English Mystics.* London: Routledge and Kegan Paul, 1981.

Rolle, Richard. *Richard Rolle of Hampole.* Ed. C. Horstman. Library of Early English Writers. London: Swan and Sonnenschein; New York: Macmillan, 1895.

Rorem, Paul. *Pseudo-Dionysius: A Commentary on the Texts and an Introduction to Their Influence.* New York: Oxford UP, 1993.

Sailer, Susan Shaw. *On the Void of to Be: Incoherence and Trope in Finnegans Wake.* Ann Arbor: U of Michigan P, 1993.

Salt, H. S. *The Life of James Thomson ("B.V.").* London: Reeves and Turner, 1889.

Schaefer, William David. *James Thomson (B.V.): Beyond "The City."* Berkeley: U of California P, 1965.

Schaefer, William David, ed. *The Speedy Extinction of Evil and Misery: Selected Prose of James Thomson.* Berkeley: U of California P, 1967.

Schlossman, Beryl. *Joyce's Catholic Comedy of Language.* Madison: U of Wisconsin P, 1985.

Scholem, Gershom. *Major Trends in Jewish Mysticism.* New York: Schocken, 1974.

Scholem, Gershom. *On the Mystical Shape of the Godhead: Basic Concepts in the Kabbalah.* New York: Schocken, 1991.

Scholem, Gershom. *Origins of the Kabbalah.* Princeton: Princeton UP, 1987.

Scotto, Robert M. "'Visions' and 'Epiphanies': Fictional Technique in Pater's *Marius* and Joyce's *Portrait.*" *James Joyce Quarterly* 11, no. 1 (Fall 1973): 41–49.

Solomon, Margaret. *Eternal Geometer: The Sexual Universe of Finnegans Wake.* Carbondale: Southern Illinois UP, 1969.

Steppe, Wolfhard. "The Merry Greeks (With a Farewell to *Epicleti*)." *James Joyce Quarterly* 32, no. 3/4 (Spring/Summer 1995): 597–617.

Sullivan, Kevin. *Joyce among the Jesuits.* New York: Columbia UP, 1958.

Sulloway, Alison. *Gerard Manley Hopkins and the Victorian Temper.* New York: Columbia UP, 1972.

Szmarnach, Paul, ed. *An Introduction to the Medieval Mystics of Europe.* Albany: State U of New York P, 1984.

Tennyson, G. B. *Victorian Devotional Poetry: The Tractarian Mode.* Cambridge: Harvard UP, 1981.

Theoharis, Theoharis C. *Joyce's Ulysses: An Anatomy of the Soul.* Chapel Hill: U of North Carolina P, 1988.

Thomson, John. *Francis Thompson: Poet and Mystic.* London: Simpkin Marshall, 1923.

Thomson, John. *Francis Thompson: The Preston-Born Poet.* London: Simpkin Marshall, 1913.

Underhill, Evelyn. *Mysticism.* New York: Image, 1990.

Vachot, Charles. *James Thomson.* Paris: Didier, 1964.

Van Laan, Thomas F. "Meditative Structure in Joyce's *Portrait.*" *James Joyce Quarterly* 1, no. 3 (Spring 1964): 3–13.

von Balthasar, Hans Urs. *The Glory of the Lord: A Thological Aesthetics,* vol. 2: *Studies in Theological Style: Clerical Styles.* San Francisco: Ignatius Press, 1984.

Walzl, Florence. "The Liturgy of the Epiphany Season and the Epiphanies of Joyce." *PMLA* 80, no. 4, pt. 1 (September 1965): 436–50.

Wilhelmsen, Elizabeth. *Cognition and Communication in John of the Cross.* European University Studies. Frankfurt: Peter Lang, 1985.

Williams, Carolyn. *The Transfigured World: Walter Pater's Aesthetic Historicism.* Ithaca: Cornell UP, 1989.

Wright, T. H. *Francis Thompson and His Poetry.* London: George Harrap, 1927.

Yates, Frances A. *The Art of Memory.* Chicago: U of Chicago P, 1966.

Yeats, W. B. *Essays and Introductions.* New York: Collier, 1961.

Young, Karl. *The Drama of the Medieval Church.* Vol. 1. Oxford, 1933.

Index

Alacoque, Saint Margaret Mary, 81
Apophatic mysticism: 14–15. *See also*
 Bonaventure, Saint; *Cloud of Unknowing;*
 Dionysius the Areopagite; John of the
 Cross, Saint; Richard Rolle
Aquinas, Saint Thomas: Joyce's remarks
 upon, 10; spiritual sight, 17; soul and
 phantasm, 23, 64, 86; Aristotle, empiri-
 cism, and the senses, 24; imagination
 and apophatic theology, 24
Aristotle: 24, 100; on light, 107
Augustine, Saint: 72, 142*n*5; manufacture
 of images, 63–64; spiritual senses, 64–
 65; memory, 101, 142*n*2
Averroes: *Tahafut al-Tahafut (The Incoherence of the Incoherence),* 87

Bax, Clifford, 90, 142*n*1
Beja, Morris, 142*n*2
Bergson, Henri: art and mystical percep-
 tion, 56
Berkeley, George: Joyce's remarks upon,
 10; *An Essay Toward a New Theory of Vi-
 sion* and the subjective nature of appre-
 hension, 88–90; perception, 94–95; as
 aesthetic model for *Finnegans Wake,*
 131–33, 134
Bernard of Clairvaux, 81
Bishop, John, 5
Blake, William, 100. *See also* Joyce, James
Boehme, Jacob: 10, 88; *The Signature of All
 Things* and the nature of apprehension,
 90–91
Bonaventure, Saint: 81; *Itinerarium ad Men-
 tis Deum,* apophasis and imagination,
 18–20
Boy Bishop. *See* Holy Innocents, Feast of
Boyle, Robert, 5

Bruno, Giordano, 47, 120
Budgen, Frank: triptych window as model
 for *Finnegans Wake,* 127
Bundy, Murray Wright, 24

Child, Ruth, 38
Christ, Carol, 59
Cloud of Unknowing: as form of psychology, 20; function of memory, 20–22;
 relation of body and mind, 22; visual
 imagination, 23
Colledge, Eric, 113
creatio ex nihilo, 11, 85, 86, 107
Compiano, Marino, 142*n*3

Dali, Salvador: "The Christ of Saint John
 of the Cross," 32
Dante: Pater's esteem of, 47
de Jesus-Marie, Bruno, 32
DeLaura, David, 46
Descartes, Rene, 137
Dionysius the Areopagite: 8, 44; Joyce's
 attraction to, 5; as source of negative
 theology, 12; *Divine Names,* 12, 15, 81;
 Mystical Theology, 14; name, 14; *Celestial
 Hierarchies,* 15; epistemology, 15–16;
 apophasis as aesthetics, 17–18; and
 Finnegans Wake, 20, 116–17, 130, 137;
 source of burning bush motif, 30; perti-
 nence to Ireland, 40; Joyce's sense of
 influence, 40–41; and Kabbalah, 87;
 light, 107

Eco, Umberto: 5; *The Aesthetics of Chaos-
 mos,* 45
Ego Dormio et Cor Meam Vigilat. See Rolle,
 Richard